Trapping and Tracking

TRAPPING
AND
TRACKING

GEORGE B. CLAWSON

Illustrated by Ron Pittard

WINCHESTER PRESS · TULSA

Copyright © 1977 by George B. Clawson.

Library of Congress Cataloging in Publication Data

Clawson, George B
    Trapping and tracking.

    Includes index.
     1. Trapping. 2. Tracking and trailing.
I. Title.
SK283.C58   639'.11   77–21593
ISBN 0–87691–198–X

Winchester Press
1421 South Sheridan Road
P. O. Box 1260
Tulsa, Oklahoma 74101

Printed in the United States of America

    4 5 6 7 8 9 — 85 84 83 82 81

Dedicated to my wife, *Gerry*, who,
through seemingly feats of legerdemain,
always managed to keep our rather
large brood of youngsters well fed
and healthy on a fur-trapper's pay.

CONTENTS

Contents

INTRODUCTION

Today scientific miracles are more or less taken for granted. Very few people get excited over fast communication, nuclear energy, or manned space flights to the moon. You have to be well into middle age to recall the time when almost no one had automobiles, electricity, radio, or television. Thousands of people throughout the world still depend on the age-old art of trapping to make a living or to supplement income. To most of these rugged outdoors people—men, women, and youngsters alike—fur trapping is much more than a sport or a way to make extra money during the fall and winter months. To them, fur trapping is a state of mind and a completely different way of life.

People trap for different reasons. Some trap as a healthy form of outdoor recreation. Even if it is only for a short vacation during the late fall or winter months, these people enjoy the great outdoors and forget about the cares and worries of life.

The recreational trappers enjoy the challenge of outdoor living. The thread of primitive instinct that stretches back to our caveman ancestors allows the trapper the thrill of the chase and the chance to match wits with wily fur-bearing animals. Extra money always comes in handy, but this has little to do with the reason they trap. Like the trophy hunter, trapping is a game that they play. These people trap strictly for fun, and as a chance to spend a few weeks close to nature.

To a much larger group, fur trapping is a more serious business. Residents of rural areas, small-acreage farmers, students, and seasonal workers, such as loggers and commercial fishermen, take part in the annual fur harvest as a means of supplementing their income. To these people, a trapline is very important because it provides them a job during the winter months, and puts food on the table.

Thousands of others, because of geographical considerations, have little choice in the matter. These people tend their traplines in the southern swamps, on the fringes of the southwestern deserts, and in the bitter cold and deep snows of the far north as a way of earning the only money they can. Many people in the United States and Canada live in much the same manner as their ancestors. In many cases, animal pelts are their only crop—the only thing they have that others will pay to get.

Regardless of where a person lives or, for that matter, the reason why he traps, all trappers use their traplines to better their way of life. Trapline profits go to pay for food, clothing, shelter, and all the other necessities of life. I don't know any trappers who are rich—and very few would want to be if it meant giving up their traplines entirely—most that I do know are well fed, decently clothed, and way above average in health and happiness. When you take a serious look at the things in life that are really important, what more out of life could any person really expect than what most fur trappers already have?

Fur is a valuable, renewable natural resource, and in its natural state cannot be hoarded or stockpiled. It means far too much to many people to ever let it be wasted. Under controlled fur-bearer management programs, trappers should be allowed to trim off the surplus fur and harvest this valuable crop.

Many well-meaning people have been led to believe that fur trapping is cruel and that trapping should be abolished. This kind of thinking is one hundred percent wrong. Cruel?—maybe. When you consider what overpopulation has in store for fur-bearers, and all other wild birds and animals, a few hours in a trap and then a quick death from a well-placed bullet between the eyes would be pretty easy to take.

Trapping and Tracking

1 | Trapline Equipment

Regardless of where your trapline is or the kinds of animals you intend to trap, there is certain basic equipment every trapper needs. No two traplines are alike. What might be needed in one place could be extra weight in another. Use your own judgment, because you know the conditions along your own trapline much better than others outside your area.

One good thing about most trapline equipment is that none of it has to be new. Since expense in outfitting is always a factor to be considered, and especially so for a trapper just starting out, many of these items can be bought in secondhand stores, while others can be easily made at home with little or no cost to the trapper. All trapline equipment must be kept in top operating condition, because no trapper, regardless of how good he is, can do a first-class job if he has junky equipment.

BASIC EQUIPMENT NEEDED BY TRAPPERS

1. WIRE-CUTTING PLIERS. Should be lightweight, with sharp cutting edges.

2. TRAPS. In suitable sizes and numbers for the animals you intend to catch. Should be clean and in good shape. New

1

traps are very expensive and good used traps are hard to find. It will pay to shop around for this item.

3. HAND AXE OR HATCHET. Lightweight, for cutting stakes, driving nails and staples, and chopping ice and firewood; also for use as an emergency digging tool. Cutting edge must be kept sharp. An axe is a dangerous piece of equipment. It should always be carried in a belt sheath or with the cutting edge covered.

4. SMALL SHOVEL OR GARDEN TROWEL. Used for digging trap beds and holes for different kinds of sets. My personal choice for this item is a World War II surplus, G.I. folding shovel, with an added 3-foot handle.

5. GLOVES. Lightweight cotton, for making dry-land sets. Elbow-length rubber or plastic, for making water sets. Leather mittens with wool liners, for extremely cold weather.

6. WIRE. Soft and flexible. Used for securing traps to stakes and drags, and also for making one-way drowning sets. Usually ranges in size from No. 9 to No. 14. Stiff wire, such as surplus telephone line, can be softened by placing on a bed of hot coals for a few minutes, and then allowing to cool slowly. This also works when using twisted clothesline wire for homemade snares.

7. KNEELING CLOTH. A piece of old canvas or plastic, 3 to 4 feet square. Used for kneeling on when making sets for wary animals, such as fox, wolf, and coyote. Also useful for carrying excess dirt away from sets. Must be free from oil, blood, and other suspicious odors.

8. TRAP PAN COVERS. Cloth or plastic in 4- to 6-inch squares, with a slit cut from one edge to center. The slit allows the

trigger to fly free when the trap springs. Cloth cut from an old pair of pants is good. Plastic sandwich bags are also good, and a square cut from fish-mesh window screen is even better. This will not soak up water, thus keeping down the weight.

9. DIRT SIFTER. Made from 8- to 12-inch square of ⅛-inch mesh hardware cloth or window screen. Used in sifting twigs, clods, and small stones from the soil covering buried traps.

10. BACK PACK OR PACK BASKET. Should be lightweight, but strong and large enough to carry a lot of equipment. Should have several easily accessible outside pockets for carrying scent, wire cutters, pan covers, and other small items. Shoulder straps should be wide and well padded.

11. POCKETKNIFE. Buy a good one, and always keep the blades extremely sharp. Should be carried at all times on every trapline. A heavier sheath knife and small sharpening stone are very handy items. Veteran long-line trappers find it much easier to skin an animal very near where they catch it rather than carry it elsewhere.

12. WATERPROOF MATCHES AND FIRE STARTER. Both are important emergency items that should always be carried. Available in most sporting-goods stores. Common wooden kitchen matches can be waterproofed by dipping the heads in melted paraffin. A dependable windproof cigarette lighter— along with the matches—adds up to some extra insurance. Small sheets of newspaper dipped in melted paraffin make a good fire starter. A small can of lighter fluid is also handy, and a small automobile safety flare, with a self-striking cap, is probably the best of all. The flare will even dry out and burn small pieces of wet wood. It can be depended upon to start a fire in a hurry.

13. SMALL FIRST-AID KIT. Should consist of small bandages, antiseptic solution, and a roll of waterproof adhesive tape. Cuts, scratches, and animal bites should first be treated in the field and not hours later, when infection may have set in.

14. COMPASS. While this is an item usually carried in wilderness areas only, it can be a very useful piece of equipment for trappers who cross heavily wooded areas or large open spaces at night, during a heavy snowstorm, or in a dense fog. In such cases, the experienced trapper might not get lost, but it is easy to get off course by taking too many steps in the wrong direction. Having a compass, and knowing how to use it, can quite often save a tired, hungry trapper a lot of valuable time.

15. FIREARMS. Every trapper requires a firearm, usually a rifle or handgun about .22 caliber; .22 Shorts are used for shooting large trapped animals, and Long Rifles are recommended for hunting small animals for food and bait. Guns are extremely dangerous when in the hands of careless or inexperienced people. Most states have hunter-safety programs taught by qualified instructors. I suggest that every youngster attend these classes before carrying any kind of firearm along his trapline. Become a trapper—not a statistic!

16. TRANSPORTATION. This can vary greatly because of the type of terrain, weather conditions, and the length of a trapline that a person tends. It could fill an entire chapter. And it can amount to as little as a strong pair of legs, encased in warm clothing and a good pair of boots, to thousands of dollars worth of specialized equipment for longer traplines.

Many trappers in the far north use ski-equipped airplanes and helicopters to fly in all of their trapping and camping equipment, plus a dog team and sled, and quite often a snowmobile to reach otherwise inaccessible areas. While few own these planes, and most hire bush pilots to fly them back and forth, these trips are very expensive, and it takes a large harvest of pelts to pay for them.

I know one northern trapper who uses a large sled drawn by a team of horses. Other trappers use expensive four-wheel-drive vehicles, while still others use canoes or flat-bottom boats. I know a Manitoba trapper who drives a small Volkswagen until the snow gets too deep, when he switches to snowshoes and a snowmobile. Others employ regular automobiles or pick-up trucks, and some who trap in snow-covered areas depend on snowshoes and skis. Many western trappers use saddle horses and pack mules. Not too many years ago, I knew a mountain trapper who covered his long line on foot and used a large pair of dogs to haul his gear. Some youngsters ride bicycles. Recently I ran across one character who travels his line on a motorcycle equipped to tow a small trailer.

Different traplines pose different problems, and what works right in one area might not work in another. So pick out your trapline, learn the terrain and weather conditions, and then select the appropriate transportation. But remember: Fancy equipment costs money, and it takes a lot of extra miles and pelts to pay for it.

17. CLOTHING. Enough of the proper kind to keep you warm, dry, and comfortable. Clothing is something that not only varies according to temperature range and humidity, but also from person to person.

One Montanan I know wears lightweight long underwear, regular work shirt and pants, and, unless the temperature gets down to about −10, never wears more than a hooded

5

cotton sweatshirt for a jacket. Some trappers, for example, those in the mild, damp climate of western Washington—where the humidity is high but the temperature seldom drops below the freezing mark—pile on layer after layer of clothing and yet always seem to be cold. Wet wool shrinks and holds body heat, while cotton and some of the acrylics stay cold and clammy. To be on the safe side wear or carry an extra jacket. If you do wear it and get too warm, you can always take the jacket off and carry it in your pack. It just might be worth its weight in gold when a sudden change of weather occurs.

2 | Scouting Fur-Bearer Signs

Many old-time trappers say that "trappers are made, not born." I agree only in part with this. I firmly believe that it also takes a certain amount of natural ability and, like a bird dog pup in his line of business, a young trapper must have a certain amount of natural talent, for there is no way to develop it.

Through study and actual experience one can learn all about traps and how to take care of pelts and market them so that they bring the best prices. While these are important, they are only part of the trapping business.

First, you have to locate the animal, and then set your traps in the proper place to catch it. The only way a trapper can locate his quarry is to develop the ability to read signs; that is, tell from a few scrapes and scratches, tufts of hair, and tracks and droppings what kind of animals use the area and in what numbers.

The expert trapper can tell where the animals are, what they feed on, and whether they live in an area or are passing through. If they are passing through, is this the route of their regular travels, and if so, when are these animals likely to return?

An experienced trapper can do this with an amazing degree of accuracy. If he is lucky enough to have a few inches of fresh snow on the ground, he can get excellent information on animal movements. There is no doubt that to be really successful, one has to have the "feel" right from the start.

Raccoon   BeaveR   Bobcat   LYNX

It is a decided advantage to be born into a family of trappers, where the older members help the youngsters get started. However, some of the best trappers today come from families that have no outdoor interests at all. In contrast to this, some of the poorest trappers I know come from a long line of trapping families. It's a phenomenon I can't explain.

Proper habitat and environment, the place where plants or animals naturally flourish, are essential to all life. They are also the key to every successful trapline. This means that each animal must have room in which to live, in an area suited to the needs of the species. All need enough food, enough fresh, clean water, and adequate shelter to rear their young and to protect against weather and predators. If any of these elements are lacking, the animal finds itself in danger. Some animals can adapt to rapid

8

changes, but most cannot. When their natural habitat is gone, reduced, or severely affected, disease, starvation, and excess predation take over.

Rapidly increasing urban sprawl is reducing wildlife habitat at an alarming rate. Some experts claim that in the United States alone at least a million acres a year are being developed into superhighways, lakes, housing projects, parking lots, and shopping centers. All of these lost acres were once habitat for wildlife. When man and his bulldozers move in, wildlife moves out into other areas.

A population shift of animals from one area to another always causes overcrowding, and unless quick steps are taken to save them, the end result is usually a slow, lingering death for many of

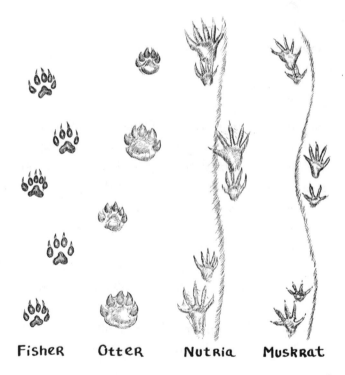

FisheR   OtteR   NutRia   MuskRat

Gray Fox   Arctic Fox   Red Fox   Coyote   Wolf

the animals concerned. When this happens—and it happens somewhere every day of the year—critics rarely blame the fence builders, the asphalters, or the dam builders. Rather, they point an accusing finger at the hunter and trapper.

In most cases, a total loss can be avoided by well-planned wild-life management programs, in which educated and trained wild-life experts—not emotional, well-meaning do-gooders—determine which animals and how many of each species can live in a given area and still remain healthy. Then a controlled reduction program, such as transplanting some animals to other areas, and then hunting and trapping, can trim off the surplus to the point at which a healthy balance is reached and maintained.

10

Feeding wildlife other than during extreme emergencies has never proven successful. Large-scale feeding programs always create new problems without solving the old ones. Instead of reducing the number of animals in an area, routine wildlife feeding programs always draw other animals, and this unnatural concentration of wildlife makes them easy prey for predators, disease, parasites, and vermin.

Animal overpopulation throws nature completely out of balance. A striking example is the elk herds in Yellowstone National Park. This park is prime elk country. For many hundreds of years, this vast mountain area, with its cool shade, clean water, and lush alpine meadows, has been the home of thousands of these magnificent animals. Due to predator control programs, both in and outside the park, the elk have been overprotected. The wolves have been gone from the park for years. Grizzly bears and mountain lions have been reduced to such a point that they account for only a few elk killed each year. Moreover, no hunting is allowed within the park.

The elk are not fenced in. Normally, when winter sets in, they leave the snow-covered high country and descend into the grass-covered hills. During these annual migrations, sportsmen from Montana and Wyoming hunt them and thereby keep these herds within the numbers that their range can support.

Under normal circumstances, this works out fine. Twice in the last twenty years this high country had mild winters. Snowfall was light, and since the elk had all the food needed they had little reason to leave the area. The normal, annual winter migration that usually caused thousands of these animals to leave the park slowed to a trickle. The elk population doubled—then tripled—and before people realized what was taking place, this huge area was overcrowded. These elk herds were actually eating themselves out of house and home.

11

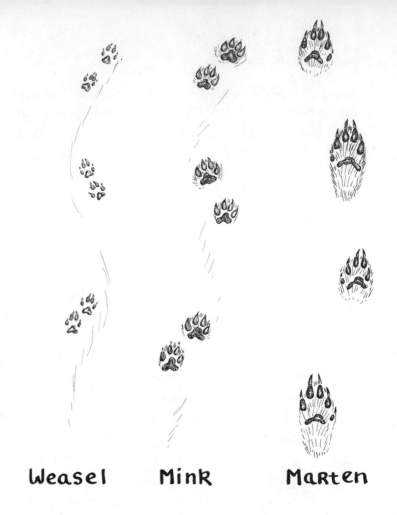

Weasel   MinK   MaRten

Disease and parasites, in the form of mange, scabies, and lice, weakened the elk and hunger took its toll. On top of this, a severe winter hit. The grass that remained was covered with ice and snow and the elk couldn't get to it.

These animals were starving, and as a result the woody plants that the mule deer and moose depended on for winter food, such as the willow, aspen, and sagebrush, were soon stripped of their bark and branches as high as an elk could reach. This caused a chain reaction. Along with the elk, deer, antelope, moose, and buffalo started to starve. About the only creatures in the entire

Badger   Wolverine   Skunk   Opossum

park who had enough food were the carrion eaters, such as the magpie, raven, and coyote.

Something had to be done, and in a hurry. The only possible solution was to reduce immediately the elk population. The decision to do this was met by a wave of public outcry that reached clear to the President and the halls of Congress. However, game-management experts in the National Park Service knew what had to be done, and they also knew that delay would only add additional problems.

In spite of public pressure, the herd reduction program was

carried out; hundreds, perhaps thousands, of these fine game animals were shot by rangers within the park boundaries. This is a drastic measure, but it is the only one that works. Reducing the size of the elk herds lessened pressure on the survivors.

Fur-bearers are not herd animals. While some of the larger predatory animals, such as wolves, coyotes, and foxes, will run in small groups during the winter and early spring months, they seldom number over a dozen animals, and most of these packs are family groups made up of a pair of adults, maybe a yearling or two, and their current crop of youngsters. These are large, active meateaters, and they must roam over a large area to fill their requirements for food.

Aquatic animals, such as the nutria, muskrat, and beaver, have other requirements. These are vegetarians that live in lakes, marshes, and streams of slow-moving water. Their food supply is made up of roots, bark, and new growth of weeds, rushes, and trees that grow in and near water. Their range is restricted to the available food and water. Since all rodents are prolific, they must be subject to a certain amount of predation in order to keep their numbers in check. Other fur-bearers have different requirements, but with the possible exception of the raccoon and coyote, none that I know of can survive a quick or drastic change in habitat or environment.

Proper habitat is the key to all wild animal population survival, and it is the key to locating these animals. If all the necessary elements that a particular species needs are present in an area, chances are good that some of these animals will live there.

Fur-bearers are creatures of habit. They will hunt near the same places, travel the same trails to food and water, and often rear their young in the same dens, burrows, or hollow trees that one of the adult pair was reared in. All of their actions are predictable. Regardless of geographical location, each species of

14

animal follows a similar pattern, and these patterns of animal behavior are what every successful trapper must know.

A trapper must be a student of nature. He must be willing to spend much time observing the habits and habitats of his quarry. Such a trapper will find it relatively easy to select the best site to place his trap.

3 | Lure, Bait, and Scent

Survival is a constant battle in the world of nature. Danger in many forms is something that every wild animal must learn to live with. Some other animal poses a constant deadly threat.

Unlike the animal world of Walt Disney and Uncle Remus, every creature in the wild must stay alert and be able to detect danger in time to take defensive or evasive action. In a world where split-seconds often mean the difference between life and death, nature has equipped most wildlife with an early-warning system, usually in the form of outstanding vision, excellent hearing, or a keen sense of smell. Of the three, the sense of smell is the most important.

Under most outdoor conditions, and especially at night when vision is rather limited, an animal can smell and identify danger much farther away than it can hear or see it. It can tell *what* it is, *where* it is, and even *how close*. And in addition to locating the source of danger and avoiding it, animals use this sense in seeking and finding food, identifying other animals, and locating a mate. Scientists are puzzled as to how a scent can blanket an area of several square miles or leave an invisible trail that another animal can easily follow.

At one time, man's sense of smell was probably as highly developed as that of the lower animals. Some outdoorsmen can detect the scent of a bull moose, elk, a big bear, poisonous snakes, and even toadstools. Not surprisingly, the sense of smell still detects and identifies the odors that are the most important to all animals —food, enemies, and the opposite sex.

The trapper who has studied the habits of fur-bearing animals is the one who has the most success, because through trial and error he has learned what animals like and don't like.

Unlike the hunter who can pursue an animal and then shoot it from a long distance, the trapper has to be able to go into an animal's own territory and place his traps in a fixed location. He then has to entice the animal to place part or all of its body into a small device. This takes some doing, because no one has ever been able to devise a method that will force a wild animal to do anything against its will. By using various types of scent and bait, the trapper provides a deception and he lets the animal's natural habits get it in trouble.

Years ago, trappers learned to mix different ingredients that would put out a powerful, lingering odor that would draw fur-bearing animals to their sets. In most cases, these worked even better than natural bait because these odors spread over a much wider area. As an added advantage, these could be made selective to draw animals of only one species. This saved a lot of time and trouble by keeping unwanted animals out of their traps.

Some of these man-made odors represented food, some a mate, sex, and others were concocted to appeal to the inquisitive nature of the animals. Every old-time trapper had his own private recipe for each species he wanted to trap. These old recipes were and, in some cases, still are well-kept secrets. But after checking into some of them—by reading old books and scrawled notes of trappers—I wonder if many of them worked at all.

Many of these lures were concocted, and still are, from the scent glands of the species to be trapped. A few drops or a dash or two of other substances were added and mixed together. When one actually reads what some of these early-day ingredients were, one is reminded of black cats, bat wings, the eye of a newt, the ears of a frog, and shadowy, cackling figures dancing around a steaming cauldron.

Early Indian trappers did employ a form of witchcraft to guarantee success for the lures, because mixing "beaver medicine" was part of the mysterious and secretive job of the tribal medicine man. It must have worked, because these old-time Indians were the best of trappers; they were the ones who taught the white man most of the successful methods used today.

Should you want to do a little experimenting, here is a lure formula I found in an old trapline book, published around the turn of the century:

"How to make decoy to capture foxes, wildcats and other animals. Remove from the legs of a horse a piece of cork. A piece the size of an ordinary hickory nut is sufficient to make one pint. Cut or shave this piece of cork into small shavings and put same into a pint of lard. Also place a piece of asafetida as large as a bean therein, and cook these three articles together. Let them boil for several hours over a slow fire. A peculiar, strong odor will arise just as soon as boiling begins. The women folk will leave the room and the dog and cat will begin to sniff and smell. After this mixture has boiled for two or three hours, remove from the stove and permit to cool. When one has occasion to use this mixture, take a stick and smear this within the abode or at other convenient places where the foxes or wildcats are to be attracted."

Two of the most common ingredients used in making modern lures is the beaver castor amd muskrat glands, and while these have strong, musky odors in their natural forms, the odors are not highly offensive to humans. These, mixed with other ingredients, will attract almost every animal the trapper wants to catch.

18

Other rather mild, even pleasant, odors that are associated with effective lures are oil of catnip, anise, and peppermint; also honey, and the extracts of lemon, orange, apple, and cherry. Some of the others, while very effective for certain animals, are not quite so pleasant to mix and handle.

Rotten meat, rotten fish, and musk from skunk, mink, otter, and weasel are also used for making lures, and while they are usually highly effective, they are also very offensive. They have a tendency to cling to clothing, shoes, and to penetrate the pores of human skin. When they do, it takes a lot more than scrubbing with soap and water to remove them. So when using these, either be mighty careful or be prepared to be a social outcast for quite a long time.

Some very effective lures can easily be made at home, but most are too complicated, too expensive, and far too messy for the average amateur to get involved with. Unless he knows exactly what he's doing, he will probably wind up with some terrible odor that will run an animal away from a set, instead of drawing it in closer.

In many cases, the ingredients used by a do-it-yourself scent-maker have to be purchased from a commercial source anyhow, so why not save yourself some time, money, and trouble by letting him do the mixing? You can then buy the finished product in a handy plastic bottle.

In the manufacture of modern scents and lures, modern science has come to the aid of the trapper, with chemistry, new distilling processes, and even artificial ingredients, that, in some cases, are much better and cheaper than some of the old ones. Various formulas are available for attracting quarry and repelling other animals.

A good source for buying lure-making ingredients, or the finished product, is the advertisements in trappers' periodicals. Most

19

of these products perform as advertised, for the manufacturers of these lures are, or have been, trappers, and they have thoroughly tested their product along their own traplines. Shop around a little, buy a few bottles, and test them yourself. When you find one that works, stay with it. However, don't expect good lure to make up for poor trapping methods.

For those who do want to make their own bait and lures for various fur-bearing animals, the following recipes are fairly easy to follow. Be sure you use ingredients that have not been contaminated with oil, gasoline, tobacco, or human odors. Mix and store in clean containers. Use plastic jugs for storage.

HOMEMADE LURES FOR THE FOLLOWING ANIMALS:

Beaver
1. Ground castors of 1 beaver
   20 drops oil of cinnamon or peppermint
   10 drops oil of anise
   Glycerin added to form a heavy paste
2. Ground castors of 1 beaver
   Oil from oil sacs
   5 drops oil of catnip
   ¼ pint of sweet oil

Coyote

1. 5 pounds rotted meat; this can be thumb-size chunks of horse
   or woodchuck
   20 drops of Tonquin musk
   Glycerin added to form paste
2. 5 pounds ground suckers, carp, or other oily fish placed in a jar
   and left in a warm place to rot (punch holes in lid to keep

flies out and let gas escape); when rotting process is complete, add 6 ground beaver castors

Bobcat-Lynx

1. 4 ground beaver castors
   1 ounce muskrat musk
   10 drops oil of catnip
   Add enough raw cat urine—preferably female—to form paste
2. 1 ounce lard or petroleum jelly
   20 drops oil of catnip

Fox

1. 5 pounds thumb-size chunks of muskrat meat
   ¼ ounce of raw skunk musk
   Place in covered jar and bury in unfrozen ground for 2 weeks
2. Rotten eggs, used in hole at dirt-hole set
   Lard cracklings, scattered in ashes at campfire set

Mink

1. 1 ounce sun-rendered fish oil (trout preferred)
   ¼ ounce raw mink musk
2. 1 ounce ground scent glands from female mink
   1 ounce ground beaver castor
   5 drops oil of anise
   Mix with sweet oil to form paste

Muskrat

1. ½ ounce ground muskrat glands
   1 ground beaver castor
   5 drops oil of catnip
   Mix with concentrated apple juice to form paste
2. 1 ounce ground fresh orange or lemon peel

10 drops oil of peppermint
5 drops oil of anise
Mix with glycerin to form paste

Raccoon

1. Canned sardines or cat food
    Glycerin added to form sticky paste
2. ½ pint honey
    10 drops oil of anise
    10 drops oil of catnip

Weasel

1. 1 small bottle of cheap perfume
    1 ground beaver castor
    Glycerin added to form sticky paste
2. Fresh poultry blood on pan of trap

Fisher

1. ½ pint sun-rendered fish oil
    2 ground beaver castors
    10 drops oil of anise
    Mix into paste; add more beaver castor if needed

Marten

1. One can cheap sockeye salmon, mackerel, or cat food
    Add glycerin to form sticky paste
2. Thumb-size chunks of fresh beaver or muskrat meat

ALL FUR-BEARING ANIMALS.

Urine and droppings from any animal you wish to catch. Remove suspicion around a set. Take these lures from trapped animals or buy from a commercial source or fur farm. Keep species separate, but place both urine and droppings in same plastic container.

Each of these recipes has been used for years by many successful trappers. Since most of them have an odor that will blow your hat off, I suggest for the sake of peace at home, you mix them out in the open air. Experiment with the recipes until you can determine the right kind and amount that will do the job.

Many trappers equate an animal's keen sense of smell with that of their own, and therefore they use too much lure around their sets. Use it sparingly. Make the animal hunt for the lure, for while it is hunting, it forgets its suspicions.

How potent scent can be is illustrated by an experience I had on one of my trapline trips into northern Canada. It was a fly-in trip into the Churchill River country, and our jumping-off point was the small Indian village of Pelican Narrows, a few miles north of the Hanson Lake Road, near the Saskatchewan–Manitoba border. The Churchill River is too far north for red fox but is at the extreme southern range of the pure white fox of the Arctic regions. Chances were slim that I would get a chance to catch a white fox, but since I was doing a magazine article on Cree Indian trappers, and would be there anyway, I thought I'd order my favorite fox scent and have it handy in case I got a chance to use it.

When the mailman delivered the scent I noticed that he was holding the small box at arm's length. As he handed it to me, I knew why, because I detected, though faintly, the repulsive odor of skunk. Upon examining the bottle I found it was all in one piece with the top sealed with melted wax. But for some reason, a tiny amount of this nose-tingling odor had leaked out.

I had to haul this bottle well over a thousand miles and the only place I could put it was in a small trunk with my camping gear. In an attempt to keep things under control, I dropped it into a small plastic bag, looped a rubber band around the top, and dropped it into another bag and secured this one the same way. When I finished the job, the bottle of scent was inside six plastic bags, and was about as tame as I could find a way to make it.

Ten days later I arrived at Pelican Narrows and though the temperature was near 40 below zero, and the trunk was unopened, there was a lingering odor. By now the bottle had frozen and broken, and while the liquid was still confined in the plastic bags, the wild odor had seeped out.

Here I was among complete strangers and not one of these people had ever smelled the overpowering odor of skunk. I certainly didn't want that first "whiff" to be associated with me.

I now knew I had to get rid of the broken bottle of scent—and fast. But how? I found myself in the position of the guy who had the bull by the horns and could not let go. Suddenly I got a bright idea. I dropped the whole stinking mess into a paper bag, grabbed a snow shovel, went about a hundred yards from the cabin, dug a hole about 5 feet deep, and buried it. As I packed the snow over the top, I heaved a deep sigh of relief because my problem was solved and no one had detected me.

This smug feeling didn't last long. Not more than thirty minutes later I heard a loud commotion outside the cabin, and when I looked out, there was a pack of sled dogs at the scent location rolling, fighting, howling, and digging in the snow. To top it off, when the dogs dug into the plastic bags a gentle breeze wafted this fragrance across the entire village.

People came out of their houses, sniffing the air. I wanted to dig a deep hole in the snow and crawl into it, but that probably wouldn't have worked either, because the way my luck had been running, the dogs would have dug me up. I was caught flat-footed, and the only possible way for me to get out of this embarrassing situation was to face up to these people and tell the truth.

But telling the truth isn't always easy, and in my case it was made more difficult because most of these Indians didn't understand a word of English and I couldn't speak Cree. But after an interpreter explained what happened, their faces lit up with laughter.

I never did get to try this scent on an Arctic fox, but if there ever gets to be a demand for sled dog pelts, I know where to go, and what to use to make a million dollars.

4 | Traps

When survival of the fittest was the only law, early man didn't rate high when compared to other animals. He was thin-skinned and his pelt was rather scant and patchy. He required shelter from the elements, while most of the other animals could live in all kinds of weather. He couldn't run and climb well, probably couldn't swim, and his teeth and claws were short and dull. While early man was foraging for fruit and hunting birds, small reptiles, and other animals, larger flesh-eating animals were hunting him, and he became easy prey when he ventured far from his shelter.

In spite of his relative physical frailty, man had one thing going for him that no other animal had. Nature probably felt just a little ashamed of herself, and to make up in part for some of man's many weaknesses, she gave him a brain capable of reasoning, remembering, and planning. Also, early man could communicate with his own kind by means of speech.

These faculties, unique to man, gave him an increasing advantage over all other animals.

Fire was probably man's earliest discovery, and as soon as he overcame his natural fear of it, he was able to use it to great advantage. Man-the-toolmaker learned some valuable lessons as he observed how other animals set clever traps to catch their food. Maybe it was the web of a spider that first caught man's at-

72952

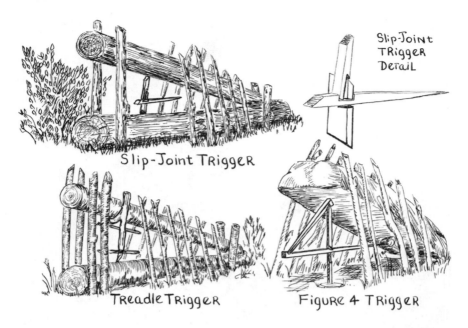

Slip-Joint Trigger Detail

Slip-Joint Trigger

Treadle Trigger

Figure 4 Trigger

The Deadfall – The Humane Trap of Long Ago

tention. If insects could make traps, why couldn't man find ways to make them?

Man-made fish and animal traps have probably been in use for a million years. The first traps were nets, snares, and pits that unwary animals were caught in. There were also deadfalls; when some sort of device was tripped, a heavy log or stone fell on the animal. All of these crude methods of trapping animals are still in use today among primitive peoples.

No one knows when or where the first traps made of iron were invented, but they were in common use in parts of Europe as early as the fourteenth century. They were brought to North America when the first adventurers reached the New World. Indeed the first business venture in America and the first crop ever

Sets For Weasel

Scent

Hollow Log Set

Stone Cubby Set

produced for export was furs, which were shipped to England from the colonies.

During the late eighteenth and early nineteenth centuries, white men began to explore and trap in the Rocky Mountains. With the opening of the West many fur companies were formed to take advantage of the golden harvest of fur that was there for the taking. Some companies hired their own trappers, while others bought pelts from the many freelance trappers who roamed the area, and who exchanged trinkets for the furs of the Indian trappers. Risks were great but the chances of exorbitant profits were greater, and thousands of young men from the East heard the siren call of adventure. They packed what little gear they had and headed west for the mountains.

Traps

Traps were in short supply up until then. Most trappers had used homemade deadfalls and snares, because steel traps were handmade and very expensive and most had to be imported from England. To fill the sudden demand, almost every blacksmith east of the Mississippi started to make steel traps.

Traps were made from patterns. Because they were handmade, each one turned out to be a little bit different, and if a part happened to wear out or break there was no way to get another part that would fit it. The only way to repair one was to hunt up a blacksmith. While every frontier trading post had its own smith, trading posts were few and far between in the big trapping areas, such as the Yellowstone, the Bighorn, and the Three Forks country.

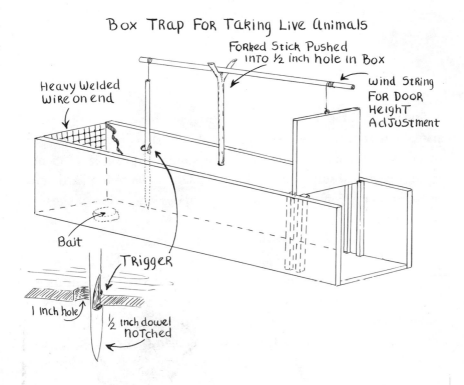

Box Trap For Taking Live Animals

Forked Stick Pushed Into ½ inch hole in Box

Heavy Welded Wire on end

Wind String For Door Height Adjustment

Bait

Trigger

1 inch hole

½ inch dowel notched

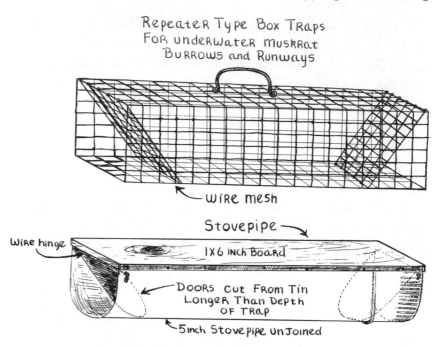

Repeater Type Box Traps
For underwater muskrat
Burrows and Runways

— wire mesh

Stovepipe —

Wire hinge

1x6 inch Board

— Doors cut from Tin
Longer Than Depth
of Trap

— 5 inch Stovepipe Unjoined

Springs created the most problems. Smiths could forge jaws, pans, and frames to perfection, but they didn't have the proper metal, know-how, and forge to make suitable spring steel. Some springs were too soft, and would bend. Others were too hard, and would break. None was dependable under the wide ranges of temperature.

These old-time trappers were a hardy breed. There is no doubt that the lure of quick riches started them west, but it was the thrill of adventure and constant excitement that kept them there. The risks were great and the chance for profit was slim. Even when there were profits to be made, the traders took most of them. More often than not, after trapping in the deep snow and subzero temperatures, fighting Indians, other fur companies, and fur thieves, the trapper found that his income wasn't enough. As a result, he went into debt to the fur traders.

His requirements were few. Regardless of whether he was a free trapper or an employee of one of the fur brigades, he dressed in furs and buckskins and took almost all of his food from the country he trapped in. However, he did need guns, knives, powder, lead, and copper kettles, and maybe a little tea, coffee, flour, and sugar. Above all, he needed traps. All these items cost very little in New York and St. Louis, but in Jackson Hole and at Green River, they were mighty expensive.

A handmade beaver trap that sold for about $1.60 in St. Louis cost the trapper $10 to $15 by the time it reached the mountains. Moreover, he considered himself lucky if the trap snapped shut half the time a beaver stepped into it.

Sometime in the early 1830s, Sewell Newhouse, a young gunsmith from New York State, put his ingenuity to work and came up with a new animal trap. At first glance, it looked like the others, but there was a big difference. When an animal stepped on the pan of this trap, it was there to stay. Newhouse's springs, made with a "secret and magical process" worked under all types of conditions. I doubt there was magic involved, but the trap proved to be enormously dependable. Within a few years, the trap was mass-produced, with interchangeable parts. Newhouse traps were expensive—and still are—but they were well worth the price.

During the early 1900s, many trap manufacturers entered the picture. By this time all traps were mass-produced in more or less standard sizes. Some of these traps were cheap; others expensive. The most expensive trap is usually the cheapest in the long run. A top-quality trap, with even a reasonable amount of care, will outlast several generations of trappers. Then as now, trappers operated on a slim budget, and many excellent traps were manu-

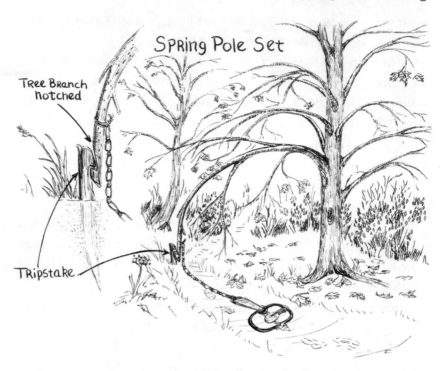

Spring Pole Set

Tree Branch Notched

Tripstake

Spring Pole Trigger

32

factured for a short time, then discontinued because the average trapper couldn't afford to buy them. Today these same traps are bought by trap collectors, who pay ten times or more above the original cost.

Primitive killer traps were produced by early man, but it took thousands of years to perfect one that was portable and efficient. There is some question about how efficient some of the older traps were. Some trappers swore by them, others swore at them. They have earned their place in history and in the fond memories of many old-time trappers.

The old Stop-Thief was the first body-grip trap that I remember, and while it didn't revolutionize the art of trapping, it did catch and kill quite a few fur-bearing animals. Some of the Tree Traps were even more successful, because if by skill or sheer luck you happened to match the right trap with the right animal, that animal slipped through the gates of "The Happy Hunting Grounds" before it even knew it.

A completely different type of killer trap that gained a limited amount of popularity during the early 1900s was the various set guns that ranged in size from the tiny .22 Short to the large 10-gauge shotgun. This deadly device was designed to kill an unsuspecting, bait-stealing animal at a range of 6 to 12 inches. In practice, the blast of this killer trap created mayhem and mutilation; it shot off legs and faces and no creature was safe in the area.

Most of these old-time killer traps are gone for good, and it is just as well. The unwelcomed destruction of these traps created a demand for the very efficient body-grip traps in use today.

The Bigelow Killer Trap, invented by trapper Merle E. Bigelow, of Milford Center, Ohio, was probably the first successful body trap. It has stood the test of time, and has been the favorite of many trappers since it was first marketed in 1925.

The Conibear Trap achieved almost instant success when it

was placed on the American market during the late 1950s. It was invented by a Canadian trapper, Frank Conibear, and is manufactured by Woodstream Corp. under their world-famous Victor Brand. The trap is made in various sizes and is as efficient as any body-grip trap can be. It is hard to estimate the number of Conibear traps in use by highly satisfied trappers; almost every trapper has a few, and the total in use is probably in the millions.

Another excellent body-grip killer trap, first marketed in 1969, is the Dahlgren Compensator, invented by Wallace L. Dahlgren, of Winnipeg, Manitoba. A few years later Dahlgren came out with a new and completely different trap, called the Shur-Pelt. Both Dahlgren traps are made in different sizes, are well engineered, and have top-quality material. The company turns out a lot of traps for the Canadian and American markets.

There are other companies that manufacture body-grip traps. While it is not my policy to endorse one trap over another, the four discussed here are the ones I, as a trapper, use and am most familiar with.

Within the last ten years, I have field-tested each of these four traps under actual trapline conditions that ranged in temperature extremes of from sixty degrees above zero, to very near sixty below. Each of these traps performed very well. Although each is designed differently, they operate on much the same principle. In order to be caught by the head or body, the animal must squeeze through it or take a bait that is attached to the trigger. Each trap has certain advantages. In certain locations, one type works better than another. However, no trap can be expected to do everything for all trappers. If used as directed, each one will catch and kill fur-bearing animals.

A snare is one of the oldest and most efficient traps for catching fur-bearing animals. Its popularity dates to our cave-man ancestors, and it has undergone few improvements since. The original snare was made from twisted vines, wood fibers, or rawhide. It consisted of a simple noose that was placed across a trail, a den entrance, or in front of a baited cubby. When an animal tried to enter, the noose tightened around its neck, holding it fast.

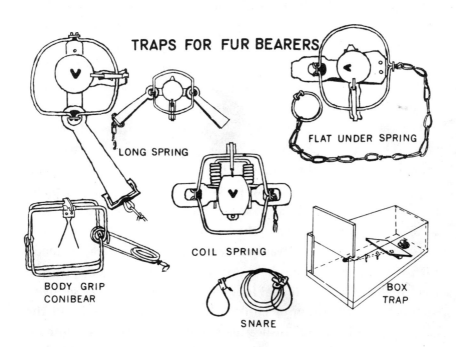

TRAPS FOR FUR BEARERS

LONG SPRING

FLAT UNDER SPRING

COIL SPRING

BODY GRIP
CONIBEAR

SNARE

BOX
TRAP

Modern snares are made from strands of flexible wire and a self-locking device keeps the noose tight. Swivels are usually added to keep the wire from kinking and twisting off. Even without these improvements, a good snare trapper can go into the woods with no more than a length of twisted rawhide, and catch an animal. Lightweight, inexpensive or easy to make, and adjustable to any size animal, the simple noose is still the favorite trap for many long-line wilderness trappers in the United States and Canada.

The snare is not only an excellent device for catching fur-bearing animals, it is also the most dependable way known to man for obtaining food in the wilderness. When the chips are down, nothing can beat the snare trap.

By using a small roll of wire, a shoelace, or even a strip of cloth torn from a handkerchief or shirt tail, a person with any outdoors experience should have little trouble snaring fish, birds, and many other small animals. With several strands of wire twisted together, one can even snare and hold deer, elk, moose, and other large game.

The deadfall is another age-old trap passed down from our ancestors, but it probably was never as popular as the snare, because it takes more time and skill to make and set up. It is a good trap and is still used in many parts of the world. Most trappers however, prefer conventional mechanical traps because they can be set up rapidly and are portable.

The principle of the deadfall trap is simple. The trap is made from heavy logs or stones held up by a trigger arrangement made from sticks. When an animal follows a trail this trap was set over, or squeezes into a den or cubby, the trigger is tripped and the heavy weight falls and crushes the animal. This trap costs nothing to make but it takes time to set up and whittle a trigger. Modern trappers are in too much of a hurry, and I doubt that one out of 500 American trappers know how to make one.

Box traps, or cage traps, for catching animals alive and unharmed, date back hundreds of years. The first one I ever saw was made from a 3-foot section of hollow log. This box trap had a drop-type sliding door attached by a string to a trigger. When an animal went for the bait, the trigger was forced out of a notch, and the door dropped down behind it. Crude, yes, but it is very effective for catching small animals. Other than for a few nails and a short piece of string, the trap was made of natural materials, and it didn't arouse the animal's suspicion.

36

Other box traps are made from wire, and they can be made at home or bought. These are excellent traps for taking fur-bearing animals up to and including large raccoon. While I have never heard of a red fox, beaver, or coyote being caught in one, I do know trappers who have caught gray fox and even bobcat in the larger box traps.

The one great advantage the box trap has over all others is that it can be used a lot closer to densely populated areas. Also, most animals are trapped alive, with only their feelings hurt. Moreover, when you happen to catch an unwanted animal, you just open the door, back off a few steps, and it will usually bolt out like it was shot from a gun.

There are many different ways to make box traps. Most outdoors magazines advertise construction plans and completed traps for sale. The box trap has not been very popular with fur trappers, because of its weight and size. However, trappers had better get used to using it, because if legal restrictions continue to increase as they have in the last decade or so, the box, or cage, trap may become the only legal trap in the future.

For more than fifty years there has been an increasing number of opponents of trapping, and their main opposition has been to the use of the steel leg-hold trap. These critics claim that trappers who use the leg-hold trap are cruel and inhumane. Instead of calling names, let's look at some facts.

This trap is the principal trap for taking the larger, more wary, predators. Admittedly, an animal caught in this trap suffers pain. But when the whole picture is looked at it might not seem as bad as some people think.

All carnivorous animals, and this includes all fur-bearers—with the possible exceptions of the beaver, muskrat, and nutria—live almost entirely by killing. The larger the predator, the more animals it must kill for food. While one cannot blame the animal, carnivores do inflict pain and suffering on other animals. Most predators like their food fresh and bloody, and they often devour the flesh while their victims are in their death throes. If this killer has to sit for a few hours with its foot in a trap, it is still a much kinder fate than it could ever get from nature. No animal ever gets, gives, or expects mercy. No trapper in his right mind would ever cause unnecessary pain to a trapped animal; if he does have to cause a little in order to stop a lot—so be it!

5 | Pelt Care and Preparation

The skill that a trapper must possess is very important. Just as important is the proper care of his pelts, lest he lose most or all of his profits. Trappers lose over a million dollars annually because either they don't know how or are not willing to learn how best to skin and stretch pelts. This is a real shame and is a waste of one of North America's most beautiful and valuable natural resources.

Not too many trappers know that many fur buyers make thousands of extra dollars each year by reworking poorly handled pelts and turning them into good ones. Quite often, with just a little soaking, scraping, and reshaping, these pelts will more than double in price. This is money that the trapper could and should have; if he doesn't get it he has no one to blame but himself.

Except when confining his trapping to the height of the season, when pelts are fully mature, the trapper cannot predict the quality of the fur he harvests. However, he can exercise proper care of his pelts. Because well-handled attractive pelts bring top prices (eye-appeal is one of the deciding factors on the price paid), a few extra minutes spent in making a pelt look good can quite often mean the difference between profit and loss.

To be able to take proper care of his pelts, the trapper needs a decent place to work. His working area should be large enough for a good-size table (usually a skinning bench), a fleshing beam or pole, and a well-ventilated place to hang his pelts for drying. Trappers often must work under less than ideal conditions and do their skinning wherever they can. However, it is best to have a room that is well-lighted, warm, and located where the sight of carcasses and offensive odors will not create problems with neighbors or with members of his own family.

The correct tools are essential for the best results. These include one or more good skinning knives, with blades of various shapes and sizes, a fleshing knife, a good sharpening stone, a tail-stripper, brushes and combs, and a supply of rags and sawdust. Also needed are a pair of wire-cutting pliers, a pound or so of nails, a hammer, a gambrel for hanging up animals, and a supply of drying boards for each kind of animal you intend to catch. Animals, even of the same species, come in various sizes, and while fur buyers require that each species be stretched to a specified shape, you should have enough drying boards to take care of large, medium, and small pelts. If you happen to catch an animal that is much larger than normal, you can make an extra drying board in very little time.

For some animals, adjustable wire stretchers can either be homemade or store-bought, and many trappers prefer these over the ones that are made from wood. Pelts stretched on these dry much faster, and since they are adjustable for different shapes and sizes, several different kinds of animal can be dried on the same stretcher.

The word "stretcher," although it has been in common use for the last hundred years or so, is a misnomer, and instead of stretching a pelt, these drying frames, or boards, should be used only to shape and hold a pelt to its normal size. It should be pulled snug and tight, but never stretched, because stretching pulls a pelt out of proportion; it thins out the leather and causes pores, hair roots, and small scars to show. While a stretched pelt might look a bit

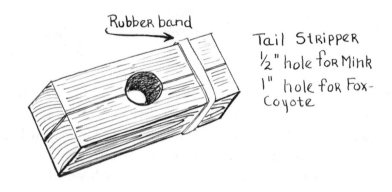

Rubber band

Tail Stripper
½" hole for Mink
1" hole for Fox-
Coyote

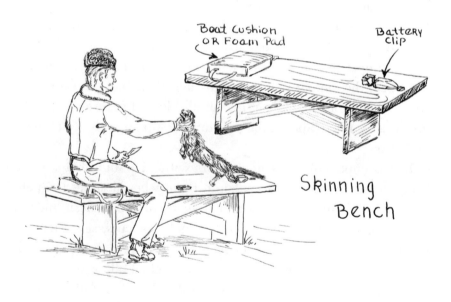

Boat Cushion
OR Foam Pad

Battery
Clip

Skinning
Bench

larger, the fur buyer will not be fooled. In many cases, what might have been a fine pelt in its natural shape and size has been damaged beyond repair by "stretching."

Animals are skinned either "open" or "cased." The open method is used for beaver, badger, bear, mountain lion, and sometimes wolf, raccoon, and wolverine. The other fur-bearers are usually cased, with the fur of some species turned in and others turned out. If there is any question about which method to use, check in advance with the intended buyer. The fur market will generally accept pelts either way, but many fur buyers have a preference and will quite often pay more for pelts handled the way they want them.

On animals that are skinned open, a cut is made from the chin to the vent, then on out to the tip of the tail. Make a cut from the heel of a rear foot to the vent, then to the heel of the other. Cut from the heel of a front foot straight across the chest to the heel on the opposite side. Circle each ankle with a cut through the skin. Peel the tail out very carefully, and then peel the skin away from the rest of the body. Wipe off all blood, because some pelts are easily stained. Spread the pelt fur-side-up and remove all mud and burrs.

If it is impossible to remove burrs without pulling hairs, leave them in but be sure not to cut into them when fleshing the pelt. Turn the pelt fur-side-down and remove all excess flesh and fat with a sharp knife. If there are any holes or cuts, sew them up carefully. If the pelt is dry, tack it fur-side-down to the board. Pull it tight, but be sure not to stretch the pelt. Follow the general outline of the pelt, and tack every 1 or 2 inches. Carefully wipe off all excess grease, and then place the pelt in a cool, well-ventilated place to dry.

Cased animals are handled a little bit differently. Make the first cut from the heel of a rear foot to the vent, and then to the other

Skinning The Tail
With The Tail Stripper

Peeling The hide over
The Carcass

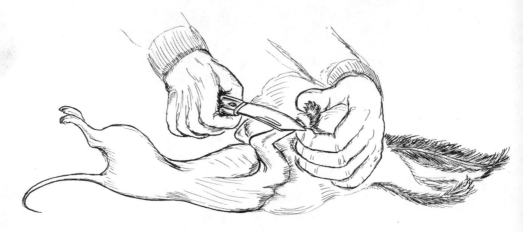

Cutting Skin Loose
around Feet

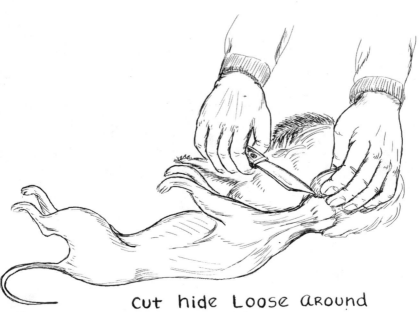

Cut hide Loose around
Eyes, Lips and nose
With Care

heel. Cut to the tip of the tail and peel it out carefully. Cut the skin around each rear ankle, and then peel the skin from the body, much in the manner as removing a glove. Peel the skin down each front leg to the ankle and cut off the skin. Pull over the head, and be extra careful around the ears, eyes, nose, and mouth. Check this pelt for burrs and mud, and then pull over the pole, beam, or board. Use a fleshing knife to scrape off excess flesh and fat. Wipe clean of blood, grease, and fat. Sew up all cuts, and be sure that the fur is dry. Pick out the proper size board, put it on straight, pull it tight, and tack it into place. Slip a tapered wedge up the belly, then hang it in a cool place to dry. A word of caution: Never use salt on any pelt.

When skinning small animals, most trappers work on a table or bench. Larger animals are hung up by the rear legs. Don't be afraid to use water to wash off blood, but be sure that the pelt is completely dry before placing on the stretcher.

Check your pelts every few days during the drying process, and each time you do, wipe off any grease that may have accumulated. Also check to see if the legs are drying properly, and pin down tails that are not lying straight.

All pelts that are cased, and to be sold fur-side-out, such as foxes, coyotes, and cats, should be first placed on the stretcher fur-side-in for approximately twenty-four hours, then the pelt should be turned fur-side-out. Leave all pelts on the boards until they have completely dried. If you have enough boards, leave the pelts on until you get ready to sell them. When you do take them off, wipe them thoroughly, comb and brush all exposed fur, and then lay them out flat. Make them look good, because good-looking furs bring the best prices.

Up until now, the trapper has been in complete control of his entire operation. Except for a few rules and regulations that he has had to abide by, he has been his own boss, and has taken care

Skinning

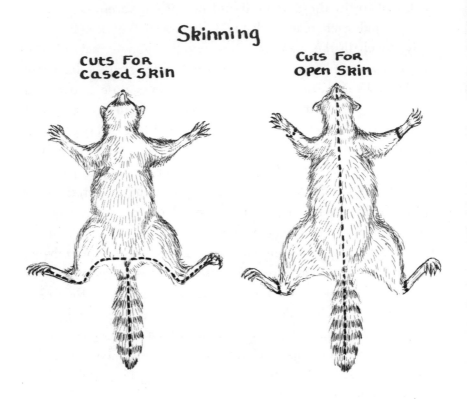

Cuts For
Cased Skin

Cuts For
Open Skin

of his trapline. If he was a serious trapper who wanted to make money, he put in long, hard hours in all kinds of weather, and he took good care of his trapline and pelts. These pelts represented quite an investment in time and money.

He is now ready to sell his product and find a buyer. When he finds the buyer, he steps right out of the world of nature and into the world of big business. Unless the trapper switches roles and becomes a shrewd businessman, with a very sharp pencil, he can lose his shirt.

Fur buyers know their business. "Buy low, sell high" is the name of the game in every business. Unless the trapper is just as

46

good at selling as he is at trapping, he'll have little chance of making a profit.

Millions of dollars are lost annually by trappers because they have no real idea of what their pelts are worth, and they sell out to the first buyer. There is no such thing as a set or fixed price for pelts; fur prices fluctuate according to supply and demand, with day to day changes. The fur buyer has many contacts that keep him informed of market trends, and he knows, within a few dollars, what your pelts will bring him when he sells them.

If your pelts are any good at all, his first bid always leaves room for some horsetrading. The best way to handle him is to let him know that you are getting bids from many buyers and that you intend to sell to the highest bidder.

I have made as much as a hundred dollars in less than fifteen

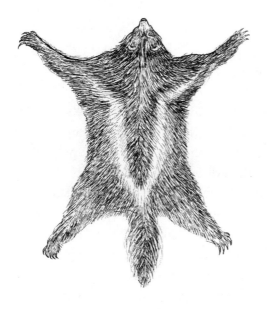

Wolverine

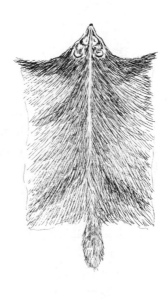

Badger

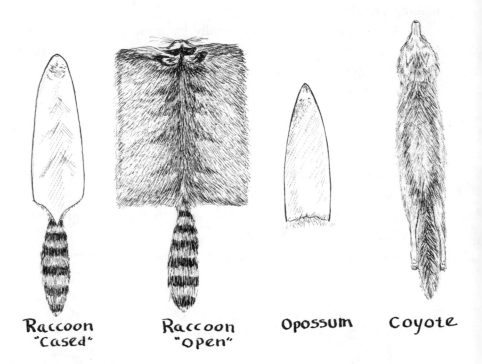

Raccoon
"Cased"
    Raccoon
"Open"
    Opossum
    Coyote

minutes by having more than one buyer bid on my pelts. There was nothing dishonest about any of the bids; it was a matter of shopping around until I found a buyer who needed my pelts and was willing to pay more than the others to get them.

When furs are to be mailed to auctions, association fur sales, or individual buyers, they should be stretched, completely dried, laid flat, and placed fur side to fur side and leather to leather. If the pelts still contain traces of grease use a layer or two of absorbent paper or burlap between the pelts. Make up a nice, neat bundle and tie it with string. Wrap them in heavy paper, but never newspaper, because the ink might discolor the pelts. Slip them into a cardboard box, or make up a burlap bundle, and tie or sew them securely. Use a shipping label both inside and out-

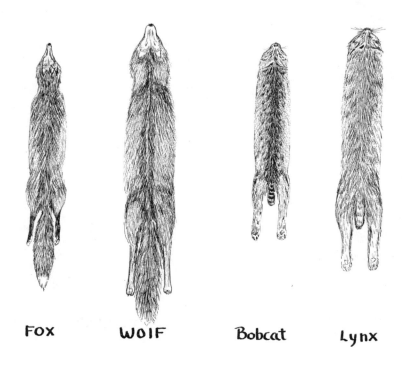

FOX   WOlF   Bobcat   Lynx

side the package, and list inside the kind and number of pelts. If your state requires special permits for shipping pelts of fur-bearing animals, be sure to follow all the regulations. Send your pelts by either parcel post or express. Since they represent quite a bit of money, be sure to insure them for their full value. Also be sure that you have the correct name and address on all labels. If there is any doubt in your mind, or if you feel that special shipping instructions are needed, always write in advance.

A word of caution: Before you mail pelts to anyone, be certain he is a reputable dealer and not some fly-by-night outfit that might take your pelts and run. Check bank references, other trappers who have shipped to him, and the chamber of commerce in his city. Make sure that you have a firm agreement in advance

49

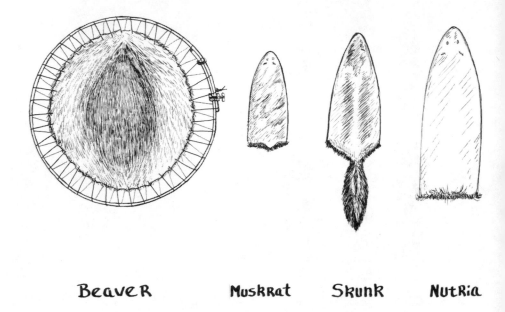

BeaveR   **MuskRat**   **SkunK**   **NutRia**

that your pelts will be returned at the buyer's expense if you are not satisfied with the price offered. At least ninety-nine out of every one hundred mail-order dealers are honest, but if you don't know who you are dealing with you just might ship your pelts to one who is not. While checking references might take time and trouble, no trapper I know of can afford to take a chance on a total loss. It is much better to be safe than sorry.

While all pelts are stretched to general shapes and sizes, different dealers do use different standards and measures in grading pelts. A pelt might be graded *extra-large* by one dealer and only grade *large* by another. If you have many pelts to sell, this could mean the difference of quite a few dollars. The only way you can protect yourself and know whether you are getting a fair deal or

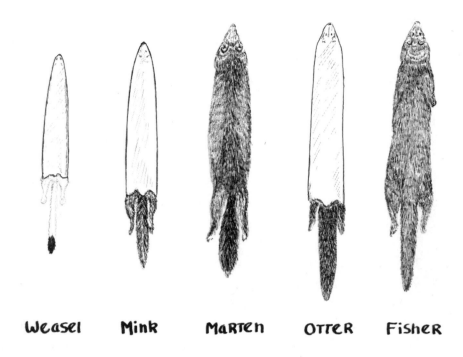

Weasel   Mink   MaRTen   OTTeR   FisheR

not is to learn everything you possibly can about the entire fur business.

Read everything you can lay your hands on. Talk to more experienced trappers. Join your local trappers' association and attend all their meetings and workshops. Get to know all the fur dealers in your area. Ask them intelligent questions, and expect reasonable answers in return. While every business is entitled to a few trade secrets, every reputable fur dealer will be glad to explain his methods of measuring and grading. If he refuses or hedges, cross him off your list.

Pelts are graded for size and quality. Fur quality covers "primeness" and the degree of damage. Some damage is caused by poor pelt handling procedures which resulted in cuts, scrapes, overstretching, grease, and burns. A lot of damage is caused by the life activity of the animal. Because of this, large pelts are not necessarily the best quality. Actually, extra-large pelts can be well down the list in quality. Large pelts come from older animals that have managed to survive traps, guns, battles with dogs and other animals. The fur quality could be affected by old age, battle scars, wire cuts, healed bullet wounds, disease, insect infestation and bites, and other hazards. While this damage can also show up in animals of any size, it is usually the large ones who exhibit the most. When a pelt is damaged, you can expect a drop or two in grade—and several dollars in price.

The following pelt sizes are the ones that most of the large fur buyers and fur auctions accept as standard in America and Canada. These give the length in inches, when the pelt is stretched on boards of standard shape and width. Beaver pelts are stretched either round or oval, preferably round for the American markets. The dried pelt is measured from the nose to the base of the tail, and then across the middle at the widest part. These two figures are added together and the result is the size.

Example: $25'' \times 25'' = 50'' = Medium.$

The sizes in the following lists are given in inches.

Beaver: Open. Stretched round or oval.

XX Large	over 65
X Large	over 60
Large	over 55
Large Medium	over 52
Medium	over 48
Small	over 45
Cub or Kit	under 45

Skunk: Cased. Fur-side-in.

X Large .... over 23

Large .... over 19

Small .... under 19

Otter: Cased. Fur-side-in. Option on otter. Check with buyer.

X Large .... 38 and over

Large .... 36 and over

Medium .... 34 and over

Small .... under 34

Mink: Cased. Fur-side-in. Option on mink. Check with buyer.

X Large .... 23 and over

Large .... 20 and over

Medium .... 17 and over

Small .... under 17

Fisher: Cased. Fur-side-out.

X Large .... 25 and over

Large .... 23 and over

Medium .... 18 and over

Small .... under 18

Lynx: Cased. Fur-side-out.

X Large .... 45 to 48

Large .... 42 to 45

Medium .... 37 to 42

Small .... 36 and under

Bobcat ... Lynx Cat: Cased. Fur-side-out.

X Large .... 36 and over

Large .... 32 to 36

Medium .... 26 to 32

Small .... under 26

53

Opossum: Cased. Fur-side-in.

X Large .... over 23
Large .... 19 to 23
Medium .... 17 to 19
Small .... under 17

Marten: Cased. Fur-side-out.

X Large .... 24 and over
Large .... 21 to 24
Medium .... 18 to 21
Small .... under 18

Coyote: Cased. Fur-side-out.

X Large .... 42 and over
Large .... 39 to 42
Medium .... 36 to 39
Small .... under 36

Red and Cross Fox: Cased. Fur-side-out.

X Large .... 33 and over
Large .... 30 to 33
Medium .... 27 to 30
Small .... under 27

Gray Fox: Cased. Fur-side-out.

X Large .... 30 and over
Large .... 26 to 30
Medium .... 24 to 26
Small .... under 24

Weasel: Cased. Fur-side-in.

X Large .... 13 and over
Large .... 11 to 13
Medium .... 9 to 11
Small .... under 9

Raccoon: Cased. Fur-side-in.

    X Large .... 30 and over
    Large .... 26 to 30
    Medium .... 24 to 26
    Small .... under 24

Badger: Open.

    X Large .... 30 and over
    Large .... 26 to 30
    Medium .... 21 to 26
    Small .... under 21

Nutria: Cased. Fur-side-in.

    X Large .... 30 and over
    Large .... 26 to 30
    Medium .... 24 to 26
    Small .... under 24

Muskrat: Cased, Fur-side-in.

    X Large .... 16 and over
    Large .... 14 to 16
    Medium .... 11 to 14
    Small .... under 11

RESIDENT BUYER Usually he operates a full-time business in the community, and buys pelts on a seasonal basis, and provides a much-needed service for trappers. Get to know him, because he is the man with whom you can dicker and deal. While you might not always sell him your pelts, be fair, and give him a chance to bid. Some resident buyers also buy skunk and muskrat glands, porcupine quills, beaver castors and teeth, and quite a few will buy your fur on the carcass and do the skinning and stretching themselves. These buyers might not be able to pay as much as some of the other buyers, but you should think twice before you go to someone else who will pay a few extra dollars. This man pays taxes in your community, and he's always available for free advice. His ready-cash service might frequently come in handy.

Lynx ~ OtteR

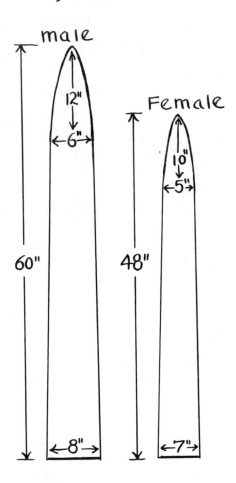

TRAVELING FUR BUYER The name speaks for itself. Unless he represents a well-known fur house or is willing to pay spot-cash for your pelts, my advice is to use caution. Most of these people are honest, but some of their checks have been known to bounce.

FisheR~Opossum NutRia

MaRten

use mink StRetcheR FoR Female maRten

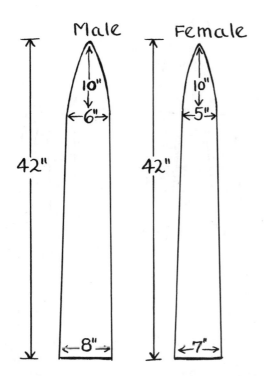

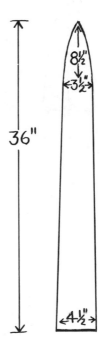

And when they do, some of these traveling buyers are mighty hard to catch up with.

ASSOCIATION FUR SALES In most states these sales are sponsored by trappers' associations, and they usually require membership in the association to sell. Sales are by closed bid or auction, and are usually large enough to draw many buyers. These sales eliminate a lot of the middlemen, and they pass their profits on to the trapper. This is an excellent way for a trapper to sell his pelts.

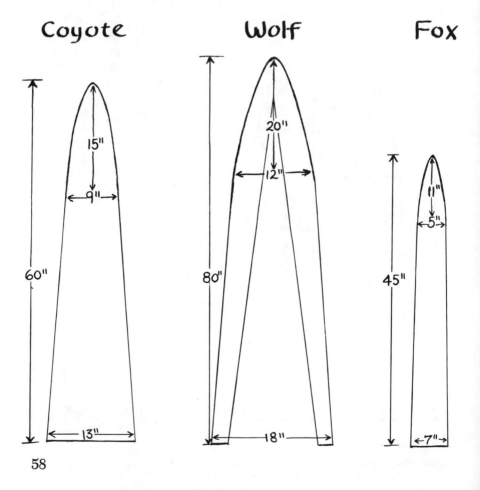

Coyote   Wolf   Fox

MAIL-ORDER BUYERS   Many of these people have been in business for years and have thousands of satisfied customers. However, make sure you know who you are dealing with before shipping your pelts.

FUR AUCTIONS   These are where buyers sell to the highest bidder. Most of the auction buyers are interested in top-quality pelts in large lots. Many of the larger auctions attract buyers from all over the world, and sales usually run into the millions of dollars.

Skunk   Weasel

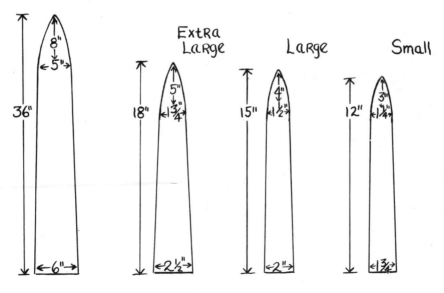

If he can qualify, it's an excellent place for the trapper to sell. Check trappers' newspapers and magazines for addresses, and write directly to the auctioneer for information.

TAXIDERMISTS Occasionally, these people will pay well above the market price for animals of exceptional size and quality. Some taxidermists will buy small or damaged pelts that have little or no market value. Check with them before skinning animals, because most prefer to do this job themselves.

ZOOS AND LIVE ANIMAL DEALERS These are outlets for unusual birds, reptiles, and certain other animals. The prices paid are quite often worth the extra time and trouble required to catch an animal unharmed and healthy. Check with interested zoos and dealers to see what they need, and with your state fish and game department for regulations concerning trapping live animals.

6 | The Mink

Probably the easiest animals for any trapper to catch are those that live in and near water. This is because the water dwellers are more restricted. Also a trap placed under a few inches of water, and covered with wet leaves or mud, is much easier to conceal from the sharp eye and the keen nose of a crafty old fur-bearer than are traps set on dry land.

The mink does a lot of traveling, and although it will sometimes range a mile or so from the nearest stream, it prefers to hunt along the water's edge. Away from the stream, it is extremely cautious, and is as hard to trap with a dry-land set as is a fox and coyote. But when it gets back to the water and into familiar surroundings, the mink loses a lot of its caution.

Like most wild animals, the mink is a creature of habit, and unless it is forced to leave an area because of a shortage of food, heavy hunting, trapping pressure, or excess predation by hawks, horned owls, or larger animals, the mink will live along one section of a stream for its entire life. It will hunt for food in the same general area and follow the same trails that were established by its ancestors.

A good example of this occurred along one of my former trap-lines, on the Yellowstone River, in southern Montana. I had one trail set made in a natural location, where an old trail came out of

61

the water and went up under a half-buried pile of driftwood. That set accounted for seventeen minks during five seasons, and the only lure I ever added was a few drops of raw mink musk.

Like many youngsters who have more ambition than knowledge, I had more than my share of trouble when it came to catching mink. After checking empty traps for quite some time, I believed this elusive little fur-bearer had some kind of supernatural ability when it came to avoiding traps. While later events proved this to be wrong, I developed a complex about this small animal that took me a long time to get over.

Later, I found out that I had been trying to trap mink where there were only a few. More experienced trappers had been there ahead of me and had cleaned out the easy ones. The remaining few I was trying to catch were trap-shy old veterans who were mighty careful where they placed their feet.

Almost every young trapper has these experiences, and as a result becomes discouraged and soon quits. The same thing could have happened to me were it not for one of the real good, old-time mink trappers who lent me a helping hand.

The lessons came hard—for both of us. He was critical of every mistake I made—and I made a lot of them. When I blundered, I got it made known in a way that I would long remember. During the first few days, I actually wondered if one of the requirements for a good mink trapper was to be half-mean and grumpy. But I paid strict attention to what he told me, and started to learn. By the end of the week, I caught my first mink, and while I had a lot more to learn, I was a mink trapper, and a mighty proud one.

I learned to read signs, and soon could read the track of a mink and other small animals. I also quickly found out that mink are never as plentiful as they seem. A lot of mink tracks along a stream didn't necessarily mean a lot of mink were living in the area.

Mink Trail-Bounding

Mink Tracks

One prowling mink can make thousands of tracks and be miles away by morning. I also learned that unless some other trapper got it, chances were good that the mink would return in less than a week. By then I knew how to make a set that had a reasonable chance of catching it.

With a little knowledge under my hat, I gained self-confidence, and after I had made a few sets under the watchful eye of my teacher, and actually caught a few mink, the mystery that had baffled my earlier efforts completely vanished. I knew that it didn't take a magician to trap a mink!

Minks are members of the weasel family, and while they are land animals, they prefer to live and feed along the water's edge.

They are excellent swimmers, both on top and below the surface, and are one of the very few animals fast enough to catch trout in the water. They feed on fish, frogs, crawfish, muskrats, water snakes, and turtles. When they hunt on land, they prey on rabbits, birds, squirrels, and mice.

Minks are small animals, but they are such vicious fighters that they have few natural enemies. Man, their greatest threat to survival, is also responsible for keeping the mink population within the available food supply.

Like many other members of the large weasel family, minks are cannibals. Very often, even a mother mink will make a meal from her new-born. Every time a mature male finds a nest of young mink, he will fight the mother in an attempt to kill and eat the young ones. However, while she may be only half his size, the mother is a vicious fighter, and more often than not she comes out the winner.

Minks are the original busybodies of the animal world. They prowl both night and day, and although they may not always be hunting for food, they are restless animals. The female has the smaller range and usually stays within a half mile or so of her den; but the mature male is a traveler and probably ranges several miles in each direction of the den. He does most of his traveling along the banks of lakes and streams; however, he occasionally is seen and found trapped in sets laid for other animals, as much as a mile from water.

Minks are inquisitive animals. They will stop and thoroughly investigate a muskrat burrow, hollow log, beaver lodge, pile of rocks, driftwood, or the source of any unusual odor that their keen little noses encounter. This inquisitive nature is the key to trapping this valuable little fur-bearer.

The mink does most of its traveling along the water's edge, so this is the place to look for tracks. Check all sand and mud bars and shallow water along cut banks where natural trails go around them. These places are highways for all animals that forage for food along the edge of a stream. They are like an open book to any trapper who will take the time to read them. A new snowfall makes sign-reading much easier, and it will give an experienced trapper a good estimate of the kind and number of fur-bearers that are either living or traveling along his line.

The mink has five toes on each foot but, while walking, only four usually make contact with the ground. They also have retractable claws, like a cat. A mink can bound 16 to 30 inches with each leap, and the tracks made by the rear feet show ahead of the front ones.

A No. 1 or No. 1½ size trap is large enough for mink, but

regardless of the size you use, the springs must be strong and the jaws must fit well together. When trapped, the mink is violent and will try to twist and chew its way out of the trap. The best way to be sure of holding these valuable animals is to make all your sets where you can quickly drown the catch. If it is necessary to make sets on dry land or very shallow water, use either a stop-loss trap, a small snare, or one of the smaller body-grip killer traps for maximum effectiveness.

It is not necessary to cover mink traps when they are placed under water, but they should be camouflaged within a few shades of either the sand or the mud the trap is placed on. Some trappers prefer to dye their traps, but I have found that a rust-colored trap looks more natural than most dyed traps, and it's a lot less trouble. I hang my traps out in the weather until they get a light coat of rust, then I hit them lightly with a wire brush, and either dip or spray them with a light coat of acrylic floor finish. Then I hang them back out in the weather to dry. This acrylic finish not only keeps the traps from gathering more rust, but it also makes the action work smooth for underwater trapping. Some trappers prefer to wax their traps, and this works fine, but it also takes extra time and trouble to apply. The process involves boiling water, and applying hot wax; it is dangerous and messy. The acrylic finish goes on cold traps. The entire job can be done outdoors, and it takes less than a minute for each trap. It lasts longer, looks better, and saves the trapper valuable hours that could be spent on the trapline.

The mink has a keen nose that can follow a scent trail over a long distance. Since minks are also inquisitive, they will usually investigate any unusual odor encountered. If its curiosity happens to lead it to a set that looks both natural and inviting, you'll probably trap it.

As well as leading a mink to food (or maybe a coy little female that might make an interesting companion), the mink's nose can also warn of danger. If it happens to locate an odor that it associates with a trap that once nipped it or in which it may have lost a few toes in escaping from it, you will never be able to draw this mink to that scent again. This is the reason all veteran mink trappers use several different baits and scents along their lines.

To the mink, some odors represent food, some represent sex, others make it fear that another mink has moved into its territory and staked out a claim. Some scents are intended to arouse its curiosity to investigate. All of these are good, and if they are used right, they are a valuable aid to every trapline.

The mink is an easy animal to skin. It is stretched cased and

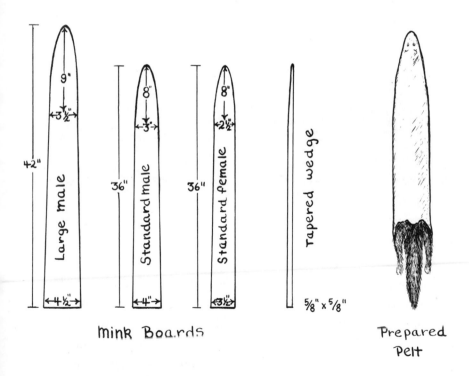

Mink Boards

Prepared Pelt

Bank Pocket Set

Bait inside

Scent

Drowning Stake

Culvert Set

usually fur-side-in; however, there is a new trend, and some buyers want them fur-side-out, and might even dock you a few dollars in price if they are not turned the way they want them. Check this out with the intended buyer. Then handle the pelts his way. Flesh them clean, but don't be too concerned about the thin layer of red flesh on the shoulders and back. It will dry quickly and the fur dresser can remove this without any problem. If you try it, you might get in too deeply and damage the hair roots. If this happens, the pelt will be docked for damage.

CULVERT SET Sets made at these locations account for many mink. The culvert or bridge forms a bottleneck along a stream, and any animal that travels in the water or along the water's edge is brought in close contact with sets made in these locations. Mink seem to prefer to go over a culvert instead of through it, and one or more spots can usually be found that will make ideal locations for trail sets. Bait or scent sets made near a culvert are also very good, because all mink that travel the stream are close enough to where they can either see or smell the set. If your lure or bait has enough appeal to cause it to stop and investigate and the set looks natural enough to arouse no suspicion, chances are excellent that the mink will walk right into your trap.

The illustrated set is almost exactly like one of my favorite sets, on Armstrong Spring Creek, in Yellowstone country. I used this same set for five different seasons, and scented and baited both sides for mink. Each year the set on the left side caught four to six mink, but never a muskrat, while the right-hand trap, less than 10 feet away, caught dozens of muskrat, but never a mink. What separated these animals, especially in a small stream like this? Why mink on one side and never the other? Try as I might, this is one of the mysteries of nature that I have never been able to solve but continue to ponder over.

Culverts usually mean roads, and roads mean people, and some people have been known to steal traps. This is one location where you should hide them well.

BANK POCKET SET Probably some variation of this set has caused the downfall of more fur-bearers than all other sets combined. It

Trail or -
Blind Set

represents the water-level burrow of some animal—probably a
muskrat. Since it is usually both scented and baited, it creates the
illusion that some animal has hidden food. When an animal walks
in to investigate, it steps right into the trap.

This set can be made either in a natural animal burrow or a
hole you dig yourself. The only requirements are that it be made
in a location where animals are known to travel, that the entrance
have enough water in it to cover the trap, and that it be narrow
enough so that the animal has to walk directly over the trap in
order to reach the bait. If possible, on all mink traps, tie the chain
to a heavy rock, or root the trap in drowning-depth water. If this
is not practical, use a drowning stake so the chain will wrap
around it and keep the mink in the water. This set is ideal for
mink and raccoon, so use all of these you possibly can along your
line.

70

The Mink

TRAIL SET   This is the set that takes the trap-shy mink. Some trappers call it the "blind set." I suppose the reason for the name is that the animal never sees it and never knows there is anything suspicious. The secret of success in making this very productive set is to keep things looking natural.

Locate a well-established trail where animals travel. If possible, place your set where the trail goes around or under some natural obstruction, such as a root, a rock, or driftwood. If the trail is too wide at the point at which you set your trap, narrow it down by using guide sticks. Be very careful to avoid placing anything near the trail which could arouse the animal's suspicions. Do not use scent or bait near this set, and be sure to keep traps and wires completely under water.

SIDE-STREAM SET   This set is one that takes advantage of the mink's inquisitive nature. The mink will always stop and investigate even the smallest trickle of water that enters the main

Side Stream Set

stream. Sets made in these small streams must vary according to the length and size of the stream, but trail sets, made directly in the channel, are very effective in narrow streams. If possible, set one directly at the entrance. This gives you two chances at the mink—one on its way in, and the other as it comes out.

The mink is one of our most valuable fur-bearers, and while it is rather small in size, it more than makes up for this in intelligence. Compared to some of the fur-bearers, it is smart, but no mink can out-think a trapper.

Successful mink trappers are not made in a week or a season. With this small animal, you have to be patient. Study its habits until you learn to think like a mink. Once you do, you'll have very few problems.

7 | The Beaver

The beaver, a large aquatic rodent, is one of nature's most intelligent and industrious animals. While it was hunted and trapped almost to the point of extinction during the Mountain Men times of the 1800s, due to study, game-management programs, and years of closed seasons in many states, now there are thriving beaver populations in almost all of the more watered areas in both the United States and Canada.

Under normal circumstances, the beaver is well respected by both humans and other animals. Its ponds provide a home and readily available food supply for fish, mink, muskrat, and raccoon, and also make good nesting areas for ducks, geese, and other waterfowl. Willows and other soft, woody plants sprout up around the water's edge and provide browse for moose, deer, and domestic livestock. Its dams also stop erosion and loss of plants and top soil in many mountain regions. However, unless the beaver is controlled by natural predation and trapping, instead of being an asset to the area it lives in, it quickly becomes a destructive pest that annually costs landowners thousands of dollars in lost timber and crops.

The beaver is pretty good at most of the things it does. It is a lumberjack, a dam builder, a canal and tunnel digging expert, a landscape planner, surveyor, irrigation engineer, and weather

Ron Pittard

prophet. It also provides fur trappers with millions of dollars each year from the sale of its top-quality pelts. The people who know it best—the veteran fur trappers—give the beaver credit for being a mighty smart animal. The beaver is one animal that tests the skill of the best of trappers, and makes them earn every cent they get from the sale of its pelt.

Like most members of the rodent clan, the beaver is a vegetarian and feeds on the green shoots of water plants, and on the bark, leaves, and branches of softwood trees that grow in and near the water. I have found a few places where the beaver has carried on its logging operations as much as 200 yards away from a stream, but this is very unusual. The beaver is built for swimming, not running, and its short, stubby legs and fat, heavy body make it extremely awkward on land. Therefore it prefers to do most of its tree cutting where the tops will fall in the water.

The beaver lives in lakes and streams, and rears its young in bank burrows or houses built from sticks and mud. Both have underwater entrances that will allow it access to its food supply, even when the ponds are frozen. Unlike many rodents, the beaver does not hibernate; since it is a large animal, it thus takes a lot of food to keep it going. During the late summer and fall, the beaver cuts and stores a large amount of logs and twigs near the entrance to its home. In a severe winter this food cache might run a little short, but usually the beaver has calculated pretty accurately and stays well fed and healthy throughout the winter.

Beavers are homebodies, and usually mate for life. Most males stay close to home, stake out their own territory, choose a mate, and then help the female raise the family. Two to six young are born in the early spring, and the young usually stay with the adults for two years. If the food supply is plentiful, beaver breed each season. If they happen to be in an extremely cold climate, where the summers are short and the winters are long, these animals will usually only breed every two years.

Beavers are compulsive dam builders, and if given the same materials to work with, very few humans could find ways to build a dam as good. It takes engineering ability to pick the right location in order to tame the wildest stream, and to know which large trees to cut so that they will fall into the stream at the right location. The beavers use these trees for a base, then add weeds, moss, sticks, stones, twigs, and other materials to fill in before plastering over with mud. When the dam is complete, it will be there as long as the animal needs it; even the wildest flood waters will never wash it out.

Thickness, length, height, and manner of construction of the dam depend on the size of the stream and the materials at hand. Some dams are only a few feet long; others measure several hundred yards. Some are built straight across the stream, while others are built with a convex curve to hold back more water. In colder climates the beaver builds higher dams so the pond will hold more water; water depth not only protects the animal from its enemies, it also keeps the pond from freezing completely to the bottom. In mild climates, where food is plentiful, winter is short, and the ponds never freeze, very few beavers build dams at all, but instead will locate a deep spot and live in a burrow dug in the side of a bank.

In cold climates, they build dome-shaped houses, either on an island or at the edge of the pond. These structures, made of logs,

Scent Set For Beaver and Otter

Scent Stick

ONe way Slide made From CORNeR BRace - Available in any HaRdwaRe STORe

moss, or mud, are the winter homes to as many as a dozen beavers. Almost every house, or lodge, has at least two underwater entrances and the depth of these will vary to the depth of the water. Once these houses are snow covered and frozen, they are almost as strong as reinforced concrete, and not even a man can tear into them without the use of a saw or an axe. Even though all the large predators in the area will check these lodges every chance they get, there is no way for them to cause any damage.

In appearance, the beaver resembles the muskrat, only the beaver is many times larger. The beaver's forefeet are rather small, with well-separated toes and sharp claws for digging and grasping—similar to hands in humans. The webbed rear feet are set far back on the body, thus giving the beaver propelling power when swimming.

The beaver has a large, flat tail 8 to 12 inches long and 4 to 6 inches wide. The tail acts as a propeller and rudder, and also as a signaling device. When the animal pops its tail against the water as a danger signal, it's not at all unusual for the report to be as loud as that of a rifle.

The average beaver probably weighs about 40 pounds, but this varies from one area to another and also with age. Since some beavers live to be twenty years old, a 75-pound beaver isn't too unusual. I knew of one Montana beaver that weighed in at a whopping 92 pounds.

The four front teeth, chisel-shaped incisors, are extremely long, self-sharpening, and are used for tree cutting, burrowing, and fighting. Although the beaver is usually a mild-mannered animal, and gets along well with its family and neighbors, some of the early spring mating battles are quite spectacular. The beaver will fight to the death to protect itself and its family from predatory animals. If cornered, it will also attack man, and many careless trappers carry marks from its teeth.

The beaver is not afraid of man and his works and quite often has ideas for improving them. It might move into your yard and cut back your rose bushes and prune your shade trees right off at the ground, and then use the surplus material to build a dam in a nearby drain or irrigation ditch. If you have a small pond or lake that doesn't quite fit the animal's specifications, it may take a notion to add more to the dam, or perhaps will dig a tunnel and drain it overnight.

The beaver plugs up bridges and culverts, floods fields, raids nearby gardens, and in some places chops down acres of corn. When the beaver moves in, it takes over. When you tear out its dams, it seems to think you're playing games and will build them up bigger and better the following night. Normal methods of persuasion will never cause the beaver to pack up and leave. The only way to stop this rampage is to shoot it or trap it.

One little-known fact about the beaver is that it is also a killer of many big-game animals and domestic livestock. In some of the western range areas, these livestock losses alone amount to thousands of dollars each winter. No, the beaver doesn't lie in wait, and then suddenly spring up and grab the victims by the throat or chase after them, hamstring them and pull them down—but it might as well because these animals are just as dead. The beaver's ponds are death traps for large animals. In early winter when the ice is thin, or in late winter when the ice is rotten, many heavy animals walk out on the ice, break through and go under, and never surface again until spring. It becomes quite clear, therefore, why sheep and cattle ranchers have little love for this animal.

Beavers are trapped in open water in late fall and early spring, and through the ice in the dead of winter. Both methods have advantages and disadvantages, but since the fur quality improves as winter advances, the pelts that bring top prices are either caught through the ice or just after it goes out in the spring. The best method depends on the trapper and the number he intends to catch. If he has a lot of beavers to take out, he'll usually start when the season opens, and then work steady until the time it closes. It's the only way to trap a large number of beavers.

Unlike many of the other fur-bearing animals, the beaver is not hard to locate. In most areas it has one or more dams, but if not there are always cut trees, peeled sticks, and slides where it enters and leaves the water. When you spot this kind of evidence along a stream, it's not difficult to find either the lodge or the burrow it lives in. Then you can usually make an estimate of the size and the number of beavers that live in the close vicinity—and decide how many you want to take out. With nuisance beaver, the landowner usually insists that you take them all, and in order to get permission to trap, you will have to follow his wishes. But in wilderness trapping you will normally take out only the adults and the two-year-olds. This means you have to keep your traps away from the main food cache, and also the entrances to dens and lodges.

SCENT SET   This is an effective set for open water trapping, and can be as simple or as complicated as you want to make it. The beaver has two large scent glands inside its body, and it emits a strong musky fluid from them in order to stake out its home territory. When the beaver smells a few drops of this from another animal, it immediately suspects a trespasser and gets set for trouble. Scent glands (castors) taken from other trapped beaver are always the best scent to use.

Find a natural location if possible, or else dig a hole or trench similar to the one used for the Bank Pocket Set. Put a few drops of scent on a peeled stick and place the stick in the entrance. Use one or two No. 4 traps, or larger, and place these approximately 1 foot ahead of the scent stick, and in 4 to 6 inches of water. Attach

79

these to a one-way slide, on a wire that leads to a 30- to 40-pound weight, placed in at least 3 feet of water. The beaver will always investigate the scent; if the sets are placed right, it will step in the trap, immediately head for deep water, and when it tries to return to the surface the slide will lock and the trapped animal will quickly drown.

DAM SET   This is also a good set for open water. The beaver depends on water depth for protection from both its enemies and the elements, and when the water level starts to drop it gets very excited. Locate the channel the water runs over, and then tear out a few sticks and mud until the level drops 6 or 8 inches. Set one or two large traps, a foot or so in front of the break, and attach these to a drowning wire, similar to the one used with the Scent Set. As

Beaver Dam Set

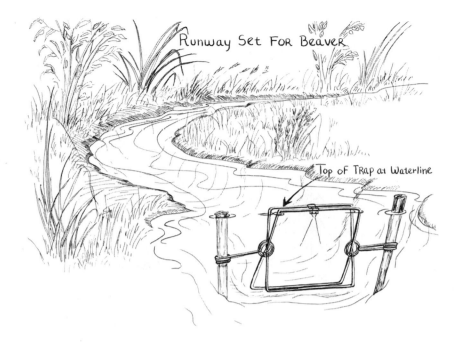

Runway Set For Beaver

Top of Trap at Waterline

soon as it gets dark every adult beaver in the colony will rush out to repair the dam. One will step in the trap, then head for deep water and drown.

RUNWAY SET   This is an excellent set for both under the ice and open water. The beaver is a creature of habit and all ponds have underwater trails that these animals prefer to use. Locate a trail that goes through, under, or around some natural obstruction, then place the likker trap, or snare, where the beaver will attempt to go through it. When it hits the trigger, the trap will snap shut on its head or body. And if the blow doesn't kill it, it will drown in a few minutes.

HOUSE OR BURROW ENTRANCE SET   This is one of the best sets for trapping beaver and is especially effective when trapping through

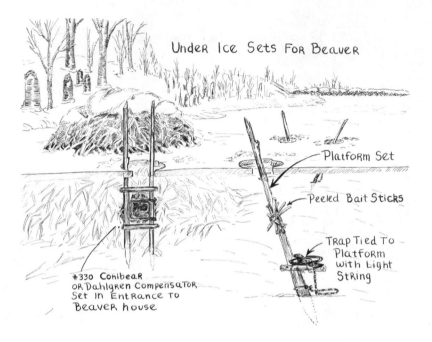

Under Ice Sets For Beaver

Platform Set

Peeled Bait Sticks

Trap Tied To Platform with Light String

#330 Conibear or Dahlgren Compensator Set In Entrance To Beaver house

the ice. Houses usually have more than one entrance, so you will have to locate all of them and set traps in each. Snares work, but the large-size killer traps are even better. Place the snare or trap directly in the entrance, and within a few nights you will catch every beaver that lives in it. In some states there are restrictions on traps placed in den entrances and near dams, so check regulations before making these sets.

The beaver is skinned open and is stretched oval or round. In areas of low humidity, the pelt is usually stretched on a 4-foot square of plywood, or on the side of a fur shed or barn. In other areas, where humidity is high and mold and mildew might pose a problem, beavers are usually stretched on hoops made of willows or metal. Flesh the pelt good and be sure that it is in a place that has adequate air circulation.

82

Under Ice Snare Set For Beaver

10 inch Snares

In my opinion, the adult beaver is one of the hardest of all fur-bearers to trap. When you are dealing with these animals, anything that can go wrong usually will. The beaver is smart and suspicious, and it takes skill and a lot of hard work to become a successful beaver trapper. Unless you're willing to spend time learning the beaver's habits, and the right kind of traps to use and where and how to use them, and then how to take proper care of its pelt, you might as well forget all about trapping beaver and stick with the smaller and easier animals.

This is not intended to discourage young trappers, but instead to tell it exactly like it is. If you plan on becoming a successful beaver trapper, expect to put in long hours and hard work for every pelt that you get.

8 | The Muskrat

In dollar value to trappers, the muskrat is North America's most important fur-bearing animal. Although there isn't as much mystery and excitement involved in trapping this small aquatic animal as there is with some of the larger ones, easy money can be made from the sale of its pelts. Muskrat prices are at an all-time high and good pelts will bring the trapper as much as $5 to $6 each. Trapping a few rats is no problem at all for even a young and inexperienced trapper, but trapping enough of these animals to make a paying proposition out of a trapline requires knowledge and planning that can only come from experience.

Muskrats are found in almost every section of the United States and Canada where there is lots of water. They range from Louisiana in the South to Hudson Bay in the North, and about all the cold-weather restrictions they have is that their ponds not freeze solid in winter.

While the muskrat is not a dam builder, it otherwise resembles its larger cousin, the beaver, in both looks and habits. The muskrat is a vegetarian and depends almost entirely on cattails and other water plants for food. Muskrats prefer to live in marshes, sloughs, and other still or slow-moving water where the food supply is plentiful. During the summer months, muskrats can be found in upland ponds, small streams, and irrigation ditches, but

Ron Pittard

in late fall or early winter, when the first ice begins to form, they will usually leave these and head for lower elevations and larger bodies of deeper water.

Like most members of the rodent family, the muskrat is prolific, and each adult pair will usually produce two or more litters of young each year. Each litter will number from six to a dozen kits. Young rats are easy prey for hawks, owls, mink, otter, turtles, and even Northern pike, bass, and alligators, but predation by animals or trappers seems to have little effect on the numbers of these animals that survive. In some areas, the muskrat's annual predation loss runs as high as 90 percent. This is a good thing actually; otherwise this always-hungry animal would soon overpopulate the area it lives in, and literally eat itself out of house and home. Then disease and starvation would take over, and wipe them out completely.

Like other rodents, muskrat numbers seem to run in cycles and hit their peak every five or six years, and then drop to almost nothing before starting all over again. Distemper, tularemia, bubonic plague, and many other diseases and internal parasites have been found in muskrats, and in some areas have wiped out entire populations. In some instances, these diseases have been passed on to trappers. If you happen to find a sick or dead rat along your line, leave it, remember where it is, and notify your Department of Fish and Game. If you happen to be skinning one and it looks suspicious, stop right there. Slip it into a plastic bag, and then call your local game warden to come and get it.

It's much better to take a few precautions ahead of time than to be sorry later, so always wear rubber gloves when skinning and handling muskrats. If you happen to find an animal that has open sores or ulcers, wash your hands and gloves in warm, soapy water, and then with a strong disinfectant.

During the fall months, the muskrat marsh is a regular beehive of activity because this is the time of year that the muskrat gets everything ready for a long, cold winter. It cleans out and enlarges its burrows, builds its houses, and stores up a food supply sufficient to last through the winter. These houses, made of sticks, rushes, and mud, resemble miniature haystacks. Each has several underwater entrances and is the winter home of up to a dozen muskrats. Before the ice freezes, the muskrat will store up piles of grass, roots, and moss, both inside and near the entrance to its home, and if nothing unusual happens, it will stay safe, well fed, warm, and dry during the long, cold days of winter.

The muskrat's burrowing activities keep it in constant trouble with the farmer, because when it moves into a pond, drain, or irrigation ditch, its burrows soon undermine the entire area. Then in the time of high water, these burrows cause many washouts, resulting in extensive damage to the land and to growing crops.

The Muskrat

In food-producing areas, the muskrat is a very destructive pest that can cause annual losses that run into millions of dollars unless it is kept under control by constant trapping pressure.

Muskrats are trapped in open water or through the ice (like the beaver, the pelt of this animal gets progressively better as winter advances). Since it will readily come to bait placed under the water, many trappers feel that under-ice trapping is the easiest and best. Safe ice allows the trapper to walk out to the feed beds and houses, which saves a lot of hard work and time, when compared with open-water trapping. However, geographical locations and weather conditions dictate the methods that the trapper must use. Personally, I prefer to use both methods. I trap through the ice when it is between 4 to 8 inches thick, and then in early spring after the ice goes out, finish the operation in open water, when gland lure is especially effective. In swamps or marshy areas, ice less than 4 inches thick is dangerous, and when it gets thicker than 8 inches, it just takes too much chopping to make it worthwhile.

The sale of muskrat pelts has put money in more trappers' pockets than all other pelts combined. And even when prices were low, profits were still above average because of the muskrat's numbers. Muskrats always live in colonies, and depending on the amount of food in the area, range from as few as a dozen rats up to and beyond the thousands. After you find them, trapping is easy, and each set that you make should be good for at least six or eight rats. I had one trail set that accounted for eighteen rats, plus one large mink, in as many nights. I probably would have caught even more rats if the mink hadn't torn up the set, scented up the area, and caused other rats to avoid it.

The No. 0, the No. 1, and the No. 1½ are all good traps for muskrats, and even a weak trap in the two larger sizes will usually hold the animal. Since muskrats have brittle bones, tender flesh, and very sharp teeth they can twist and chew their way out of a trap in a hurry. The only way to be sure of holding a rat in a conventional trap is to drown it as quickly as you can. This is simple. All you do is push a stake into the bottom, in drowning-depth water. The rat will wind the trap chain around this, and the weight of the trap will quickly pull it to the bottom.

For shallow-water trapping, stop-loss traps or the small size killer traps are very effective. And in runways or burrows, the old "stove-pipe trap" or one of the more modern cage-type repeater traps will often catch and drown six to a dozen rats at a time.

BANK POCKET SET   For open-water trapping, this is one of the good ones. Made similar to the one for mink, but in the fall or winter scented with a food lure, and a carrot, parsnip, or slice of apple for bait—or during the early spring breeding season,

TRap Sets FoR Muskrat

Scent on Stick

Drowning Stake

Humane TRaps in Entrances OF Muskrat House

Shallow Water Set With Stop-Loss TRap

88

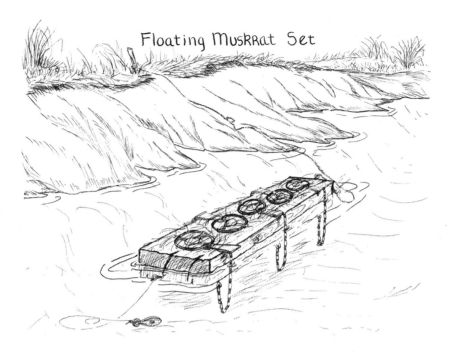

Floating Muskrat Set

scented with gland lure—this set will draw and catch every muskrat in the area. Keep the trap under water in the entrance, and be sure and use the drowning stake. Waterfowl are also attracted to this bait, so in areas where wintering ducks are a problem, use a small hole and set the trap inside, or use scent only.

FLOAT SET   This is another good set for open water, and has advantages over some of the others because it can be used in deep water, or water of varying depth caused by rainfall or tides. This set can be made on a floating log or plank of almost any size that suits the trapper. Anchor it to the bottom or tie it to the bank. Scent and bait it, add the number of traps you want, tie these to the bottom of the float, and cover them lightly with moss or grass. When the rat gets in one, it will dive off the float, and the weight of the trap will keep it under until it drowns.

Killer Trap Set   Under Ice Set

Sets For Muskrat

MUSKRAT HOUSE SET   This set can be used for either through the ice or open-water trapping. Each muskrat house is usually 6 or 8 feet across the bottom and rounds off at the top, at approximately 3 feet in height. All houses have several underwater entrances with well-worn runways that lead to them. Place small killer traps in the entrances and use the cage or stovepipe traps in the runways. The tops of these houses are also good places in which to place traps for otter, mink, raccoon, and fox. They are also good resting places for predatory birds and waterfowl, so place a few upright sticks in the top to discourage these birds from landing. Some states prohibit muskrat trapping in or near these houses; check with your game warden before making sets in these locations, just to be on the safe side.

90

UNDER-ICE BAIT SET   This set usually consists of no more than a dry pole, pushed through a hole cut in the ice and then shoved into the mud at the bottom of the pond. With a trap placed on a small platform or tied directly to the pole with a light string, a carrot, parsnip, or slice of apple is tied to the pole, 4 to 6 inches above the trap. The small Conibear is very effective with this set. Tie several of these traps to the pole, and tie the bait directly to the trigger. Make this set in several feet of water. In an area where you know muskrats live and feed, and where you expect your traps to be full almost every time you tend them, be sure and use a dry pole. If you use a green one and a hungry beaver happens to swim by, it'll cut it off, and drag off trap and all.

Skinning, fleshing, and stretching a muskrat is easier than trapping it, and an experienced trapper can do the entire operation in less than ten minutes. Muskrats are skinned cased, the tail is cut off and discarded, the pelt is scraped to get off excess flesh and fat, and then placed fur-side-in on the stretcher to dry. Be sure that the fur is completely dry before pulling on the stretcher. Wire stretchers work exceptionally well with muskrat pelts, and will usually dry within two or three days.

The muskrat is easy to locate, easy to trap, easy to skin and stretch. Above all, at the present time, it's easy to sell because the fur buyers want all the good muskrat pelts they can get. For the first time in years fur prices favor the trapper—and old brother muskrat is sitting right on top of them all.

9 | The Raccoon

The raccoon, a 20- to 35-pound member of the bear family, is found in almost every section of the United States and in the southern half of most of the Canadian provinces. It is a land animal and is nocturnal in its habits.

If I had to pick one animal that I thought was the most outstanding example of all North American wildlife, I wouldn't hesitate one minute in choosing the raccoon for the honors. Not that the raccoon's heavy pelt is the most valuable or that this animal is even as smart as some of the others, but rather because it is tough, tenacious, and one of the most versatile animals on the face of the earth. Due to this the raccoon can thrive and even increase its numbers in many areas where less fortunate animals would soon starve to death. The raccoon seems to carry its own "proper environment" around with it, and wherever it decides to set up housekeeping the area quickly becomes good coon country.

Elevation, low temperatures, and even deep snow seem to have little effect on where the coon can live. It's equally at home in the tideland marshes of Florida and in the ice-cold waters, fifty-below-zero temperatures, and 10-foot snowdrifts in Yellowstone National Park. When extreme weather conditions restrict its outdoor activities, the raccoon goes into semihibernation and lives off its many layers of fat until the weather warms up again.

The Raccoon

Most raccoons prefer to live and feed near the water's edge, but some live on the high ridges in the backcountry, and still others live along the fringes of deserts, where water is scarce. They den in hollow trees, abandoned badger and beaver burrows, rock piles, and even under farm buildings. All can swim like a duck, run like a fox, climb like a cat, fight like a demon, and can eat and grow fat on almost anything that they can find.

The raccoon is a prolific animal and has from four to eight young each season. The females are good mothers, and will fight to the death to protect their young from predatory birds and animals. The old males seem to be solitary, traveling animals, and have no family ties or responsibilities.

All raccoons eat fish, frogs, shellfish, nuts, fruits, and berries, and they are not above stripping a farmer's field of roasting ears, strawberries, and watermelons. At the first opportunity, a raccoon will also slip into a hen house and clean out all the eggs and several chickens with each visit.

The adult raccoon has few natural enemies; about the only one that is a serious threat is man. Coon hunters catch thousands of these animals each winter. Trappers catch even more. Surprisingly, automobiles probably kill more coons than hunters and trappers together. Coons have a habit of feeding on road-killed birds and animals at night. Bright headlights blind them, and they just can't move fast enough to get out of the way.

Young raccoons have a number of enemies, most of which are encountered during their nighttime training sessions when their mothers are teaching them to hunt and fish. No matter how protective the mother is, foxes, bobcats, horned owls, and alligators always manage to catch a few of these young coons. Probably their most serious threat comes while the young ones are still in the nest. Few people realize that tree-climbing ants kill thousands of young coons each year. These tiny meat-eaters swarm up the den trees and eat the young coons alive. Try as she might, the mother is helpless, because there is just no way to defend her young against untold thousands of these quarter-inch killers.

The average raccoon is mild-mannered, good-natured, and seems to get along with most of its animal neighbors. However, for some unknown reason, it hates the mink and will kill and completely destroy every mink it happens to find. If a coon finds a mink alive in a trap, the trapper will be the loser.

Raccoons in general are smart animals, but they have one failing that always gets them into trouble: they are not afraid of anything, including man. They never take danger seriously and seem to think it is a game instead of a threat to their life. Instead of avoiding man, his outbuildings, highways, hen coops, and gardens, the coon regards these as a supply of fine food, maintained especially for itself. It has little fear of traps, and when it finds a set that has bait to its liking, it will stay right there and keep on trying until it either gets caught or steals the bait. And even if it does get a toe pinched, and then manage to get away, chances are it will be right back to the same set the following night. The raccoon really has a one-track mind, and this makes trapping it easy.

Probably more raccoons are trapped by accident than on purpose. This animal covers a lot of territory on its nightly forays. It has a keen sense of smell and can detect odors over a long distance. When this is combined with an insatiable curiosity that causes it to investigate every unusual odor, and especially one that it associates with food, the raccoon is caught in many traps set for other animals.

The Dirt Hole Set, made for fox and coyote, and almost any kind of a bait set made for other animals accidentally catch a lot of coon. When trapping for mink along the water's edge, the Bank Pocket Set and the Trail Set are just as good for coon as they are for the smaller animal. Up until the last few years this created a serious problem for mink trappers.

Mink and raccoon live and hunt in the same general area. At one time, when mink prices were high and coon pelts were almost worthless, it seemed that the best way to catch one of these masked bandits was to spend thirty minutes or so in making a good mink set. You were almost sure to catch a coon in it the first night. And when you did, you were obliged to move the set to another location because after it had once caught a coon, a mink would never come near it.

Because of this, many trappers tried to trap most of the coon off their lines before the mink season opened. But now that fashion trends have reversed, and raccoon pelts are selling for extremely high prices, this former trapline nuisance is the one most trappers want to catch these days.

The Bank Pocket Set and the Trail Set, illustrated in the chapter on mink, are also excellent sets for raccoon, with the only suggested changes being larger-size wire and more care in tying the traps. The raccoon is a strong animal and will make every effort to get away by chewing on the wire and every stake, branch, or root it can reach. If it happens to chew one in two, and your trap is tied to it, both trap and coon will quickly vanish. I suggest that you tie to something at least as large as your wrist. Better yet, tie the trap to sturdy stakes, rocks, or roots completely under the water.

Many coon trappers make the mistake of using traps that are too large. Large traps break bones and cut off blood circulation, and the foot soon becomes numb and loses its feeling. When this happens, the coon will chew off the foot and get away. Not only is this cruel to the animal, but it also causes the trapper to lose a valuable pelt. If you must use large traps, use those with off-set jaws, with a gap of $\frac{3}{16}$ to $\frac{5}{16}$ inch between them. And if these are not available, use a turn or two of soft No. 9 wire around the jaws of a conventional trap, to get the correct spacing.

Off-set jaws cause the raccoon little pain, and don't cut off circulation. The coon will not chew on its foot, because when it does, this causes more pain than the trap. Small traps, such as the No. 1 and No. 1½, are large enough for coon, and since they hurt the coon very little, it won't try half as hard to escape. When it learns that it can't get away without hurting itself, it will usually eat all the bait that it can find, and then curl up and go to sleep.

The raccoon is the original busybody of the animal world and it is inquisitive about almost everything that it encounters. It always seems to have time to stop and investigate shiny pebbles or tin cans, floating logs, hollow logs, and any hole along the bank that might contain a water snake, a crawfish, or a frog. Shiny things seem to fascinate the coon the most, especially when the bright object happens to be under a few inches of rippling water. The Mirror Set takes advantage of the coon's natural instinct, and almost always gets results. Make this set where a well-traveled trail runs along the water's edge.

Tie a small mirror or a shiny piece of tin to the pan of a No. 1 or No. 1½ size trap. Place the trap under 2 to 6 inches of water and in an open area where moonlight can strike it. Tie the trap to a root or stake under water. The coon will see the shiny pan and reach down to investigate; the trap will spring and catch it by the foot.

Sets For Raccoon

Bait in hollow

Bait in hole

Hollow Tree Set

Bank Pocket Set

Flasher Set   This is probably the best raccoon set ever invented, and it is just as good for red fox, mink, and otter. This set also takes advantage of an animal's natural habits of feeding in and along the water, and its curiosity about moving, flashing objects. Since you never know in advance what size of animal will come to this set, it is always a good idea to use larger than average traps.

Locate a shallow riffle in a fast-flowing stream, where you know animals feed and travel. Drive a strong stake into about 6 to 8 inches of water, and leave 4 to 6 inches of the stake above the surface. Use several drops of mink, otter, or fox lure on top of the stake. Tie a bright fishing lure—without hooks—a bright can lid, or other shiny object to about 1 foot of string, and tie it to the stake so it shimmers and dances on the surface. Place two No. 2 or No. 3 size traps downstream, approximately 12 to 16 inches below the flasher, and tie these to separate heavy stones or stakes. The animal will smell the lure, and when it investigates to see where the odor is coming from, it will locate the flashing object in the water. Its curiosity will do the rest. It will always wade in from below the set and grab at the twisting, turning, tantalyzing flasher. While doing this, it will step right into the trap. Since the trapped animal is kept out in the current, it will tire and drown within a very short period of time.

Baited cubby sets, made in the base of hollow trees or hollow logs along the bank, make good sets for raccoon, and some of the larger body-grip killer traps work well in these. Use fresh fish, sardines, cat food, or almost any kind of meat for bait. Use a few drops of raccoon or mink scent near the entrance. Every raccoon that happens by will stop and investigate, and walk into the traps.

The traditional way of handling raccoon pelts was to use the open method when skinning, and then tack them to the side of the barn or lace them to a frame and attempt to stretch them square. If you've never tried this, there is no way to begin to explain the problems involved. The fur market now prefers raccoon pelts cased and dried fur-side-in.

The coon is not a hard animal to skin, but since it is a large animal and has a tough skin, it takes a lot of man power to peel the skin off. It's a good idea to make the initial cuts, skin out around the rear feet, legs, and tail, and then hang the animal up by one or both rear feet, so that you can add a little of your weight when you do the peeling. Young coons are easy to peel, but some of the older animals are so tough that you almost have to cut the skin from the carcass. Leave as much of the fat on the carcass as you possibly can. This saves time later, because all that remains on the pelt will have to come off during the fleshing part of the operation.

After the skinning job is completed, turn the skin fur-side-out and remove all mud, blood, and burrs. Then turn the skin fur-side-in and pull it on the board that you intend to stretch it on.

Check for old scars that might have formed ridges, and also for any bumps that might indicate a burr that was missed, because if you happen to hit one of these, it will cut a large hole and damage the pelt. Using a sharp knife, start at the head, lay the blade flat on the skin, and then pull it toward you with long, even strokes. If it's done right, the fat will shave off right down to the leather. When most of the heavy fat is off, use the fleshing knife to scrape and finish the job. Use a dry rag to wipe off all excess grease. Pull the pelt tight on the board, tack it in place—be sure that the tail is ripped all the way to the tip—and then hang it in a well-ventilated place to dry.

Top-quality, well-handled raccoon pelts sell for as much as $60 each, while greasy poorly stretched pelts are almost worthless.

Other than size, most of the wide range in price is due to the way pelts are taken care of. After the trapper goes to all the hard work in order to catch these animals, it makes good business sense to spend a little extra time on the pelts—to more than double the price he receives.

10 | The Coyote

The coyote, or prairie wolf, is one of nature's most indestructible creatures and continues to thrive in spite of man's best efforts to wipe this animal off the face of the earth. And like the common housefly, when you swat one coyote down at least a dozen more, larger, stronger, and even smarter coyotes seem to spring up out of nowhere to take its place.

The coyote has cost taxpayers more money than all of the other predators combined, because millions, and probably even billions, of dollars have been spent by individuals, stockmen's associations, and various branches of both the U.S. and Canadian governments in an effort to eradicate or at least control this predatory animal. And while they have poisoned millions, shot thousands, and even managed to trap a few, about all they have actually accomplished for all this money and effort has been to make the coyote spread its range in all directions. Now, instead of being more or less restricted to the western prairies, sightings of these animals are being reported from all parts of the country, even in the suburbs of some of our larger cities. One thing is certain: when you see one coyote in the daytime there are at least a dozen more hid back in the brush that only travel and hunt during the hours of darkness.

Make no mistake about it—the coyote is a serious predator

Ron Pittard

when it moves in close to populated areas. This animal is a blood-thirsty killer that preys on all kinds of wildlife and domestic live-stock as well. If it gets a chance it will cut a wide swath of death and destruction through bands of sheep, flocks of poultry, and even new-born calves and colts. Once the coyote finds that do-mestic animals are much easier prey than the wild ones, hunting them soon becomes a habit. The only way to stop the coyote is to kill it. If it happens to be one of the trap-shy old-timers—and it usually is—this job will never be easy.

Since many coyotes have spent their entire lives dodging man, his dogs, his guns, and his traps, they seem to have developed an

102

almost uncanny ability when it comes to avoiding trouble. Many of these old veterans are much better at detecting traps than most trappers are at setting them. This animal lives entirely by its wits. Like it or not, we might as well get used to seeing it around, because like the lowly cockroach, we'll probably have coyotes forever.

Coyotes are carnivorous animals and prefer to kill most of their food for themselves, but they will also eat any dead animal they happen to find, including other coyotes. The coyote's main diet is made up of mice, rabbits, ground nesting birds, prairie dogs, gophers, and the young of larger animals, including elk, deer, antelope, and even moose. Coyotes run in packs during the winter months, and these packs can easily kill a full-grown, big-game animal in healthy condition, such as deer. Each year, these packs kill and eat deer by the thousands. And when coyote populations are up, deer populations are always down. In some areas, the deer population is dropping at an alarming rate, and in some marginal areas has almost reached bottom. Even in some of the top deer producing states, such as Wyoming and Montana, the deer population is about half of what it was ten years ago.

Coyotes usually breed in January or February, and from four to eight young are born in June. Most of their dens are dug under rock ledges, in enlarged badger burrows or other holes in the ground. This is a time when the female coyote wants isolation, and these dens are usually several miles away from the nearest populated area. She stays near the den for the first several weeks, and depends on her mate to bring food for both her and their family of young coyotes.

The male coyote is a good provider, and almost every night brings birds, rabbits, and other small animals to the entrance of the den and turns them over to the female. She seems to be appreciative and rather affectionate but doesn't trust the male completely, and for the first few weeks, if he tries to enter the den, she will show her teeth and warn him away. But after the young coyotes get their eyes open and play outside the entrance, they seem to become one big happy family, with both adult animals constantly alert for any possible danger. Both adults seem to share the responsibility of teaching the young to hunt, and how to make their way in a hostile world where every man is against them. As soon as this training period is completed, the male has fulfilled his family obligations and takes off for a life of his own. The young coyotes usually stay with the mother and hunt in a family group, or pack, through their first fall and winter. During the spring breeding season, they break away from the family group and start families of their own.

Sooner or later, almost every trapper will get a chance to match wits with the coyote. Coyote trapping is always a challenge, and the trapper has to be willing to spend a lot of time in studying its habits. To be successful, you must know how the coyote thinks, and then use every advantage you can.

Contrary to common belief, the coyote is not afraid of the odor of metal or humans, but if it thinks there is the slightest chance of danger, it will quickly leave the area. The coyote will come right into your yard, dump your trash barrel, eat out of your garbage can, and seem to think nothing of it, but if you happen to leave a little human odor near a dead animal that it is in the habit of feeding on, its instinct for danger will make it think "traps" and warn it to stay away.

Like all animals, and even some humans, the coyote can concentrate on only one thing at a time. The most successful way to trap this animal is to take advantage of this weakness and snap the trap on it while its attention is being diverted by something else. A coyote always has to eat. A set made in an area where it hunts for food or near an available food supply such as the car-

104

cass of a dead horse or cow gives the trapper a tremendous advantage over this wily animal.

DIRT HOLE SET   This is probably the best set there is for both coyote and fox. It takes advantage of the habit of all members of the canine family to bury surplus food with the intention of digging it up later. Every animal that finds one of these coyote "food banks" feels that this is a good chance to freeload a meal. And while the animal has its mind on the trick it is playing, the trapper can be playing a few tricks of his own.

Even an inexperienced trapper can make this set and have a reasonable chance of catching a coyote. Just make sure the traps are completely out of sight, and that you leave no human odors or tracks in the area. The coyote is not afraid of these, in places

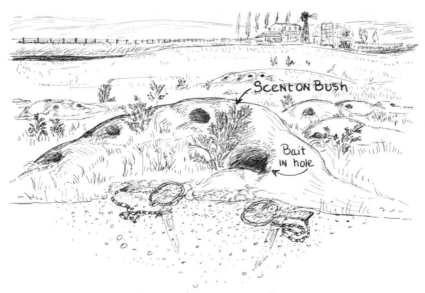

The DiRt Hole Set

where they are to be expected, but another animal was supposed to have buried this food, and man-smell around it makes the coyote suspicious.

The coyote is rattled by sudden surprises, so if at all possible, it prefers to feed in wide-open spaces where it can concentrate on eating, and not have to worry about a man or another animal getting in too close. Open areas, such as fields or pastures, or, best of all, gopher or prairie dog towns, make the best location for the Dirt Hole Set. Every coyote in the vicinity knows where these small animals live, and visits these towns at frequent intervals. And since the coyote expects to find food here, and also the odor of other animals of its own species, its suspicions are lulled.

Locate an abandoned mound, preferably one with a shallow hole already in it, or dig a small hole of your own. Make it about 4 inches across the entrance, and 6 to 8 inches deep. Spread the excess dirt in a fan-shaped pattern directly in front of the hole. Use prepared coyote bait in the hole, and then lightly cover with grass. Use a few drops of coyote scent or raw urine on a nearby rock or bush. Be sure to wear clean gloves when handling traps or bait to avoid leaving any human scent on these items.

One trap will work, but two will more than double your chances. Dig locations for these approximately 8 to 12 inches in front of the hole. Wire a metal stake to the trap chain, and drive this into the trap location so that when everything is in place, the trap will sit directly over the stake. Shorten the chain with an S hook until it is only 6 to 8 inches long. Use No. 3 or No. 4 size traps, and bed these in until the pan is just below the surface (a trap pan cover will keep loose dirt from clogging the action). Use the dirt sifter, and place about ¼ inch of dirt over the trap. The coyote expects the dirt to be disturbed at this kind of location, and it might even be suspicious if it isn't. Leave the excess dirt there, but use a weed to brush away your tracks when the set is completed. A well-made Dirt Hole Set is a catchall, and will snarl

TRail Set FoR Coyote

bobcats, badgers, skunk, raccoon, and even the farmer's dog. So with good public relations in mind, always be sure to make this set in isolated areas only.

TRAIL SET   The coyote uses the same general trails, usually made by big-game animals or livestock, when searching for food or when traveling from one area to another. If you locate a trail that has enough coyote tracks in it to indicate regular use, look around until you find a good place to make the set. Try to find some kind of bottleneck, possibly a place where the trail goes around a fence corner or skirts a thick patch of brush or a pile of large rocks. Then if you can find some kind of natural obstruction that the animal has to step over, such as a fist-sized stone, a tree branch, or an old fence post, this is the place to make the set. If you can't

Scent Post Set

FOX OR COYOTE
URINE ON POST

find anything in the trail that fits the need, place something in or across it. This is very important. The animal has its mind on the obstruction, and at this time it isn't too careful where it places its feet. Also, when it steps over something, it steps down hard. This causes the trap to catch it high on the foot.

Two large traps are usually used with this set, one on each side of the object the animal steps over. Use a kneeling cloth when making this set, and carry away the excess dirt in the cloth.

Dig a trap bed in so that the trap pans will be approximately 6 inches on either side of the object. Make the bed deep enough to hold a stake or a grapnel, and place the traps directly on top of this. Use the pan cover, and sift about ¼ inch of dirt over the

108

trap. Brush out all marks and remove the excess dirt from the immediate area. Use no scent or bait; the secret of success to the Trail Set is to keep the area natural. At times, big-game animals and livestock may cause thrown traps, but since their stride is longer than that of the coyote, most of these animals will usually step over. This set will also catch dogs, so post notices for hunters, and make it in isolated areas only.

SCENT POST SET This set takes advantage of a habit that all members of the canine family have. None of these animals, including the dog, can ever resist the chance to leave a few squirts of urine on every prominent object. An old post, standing alone in open country, seems to be a message center for every coyote for miles around. If you can't locate one that has been used for years,

Trench Set

then set up a post of your own, preferably near a location where two well-used trails cross.

Give the post a shot of raw coyote urine about once a week, for at least a month. By this time, every coyote in the vicinity should be using it. I also like to have my drags in position well in advance of setting traps so the coyotes will get used to seeing them, and not get suspicious. These drags are usually old fence posts, and will let a trapped coyote leave the immediate area of the set, but will hang up in the first patch of brush that it tries to go through.

Use two traps at this set. Dig the trap beds into the place that shows the most tracks. Use the same methods used with the other sets: take all excess dirt away from the set, do not walk in the trail when approaching this set, and each time you check it, give the post a generous application of raw coyote urine.

Most of the time I prefer to stake my coyote traps solid, but the Scent Post Set is the one exception. Several coyotes might visit this set each night, and there is always a good chance for a double catch. The reason I prefer old posts instead of grapnels is that the posts work for guide sticks. When these are placed about 2 feet out from the post, the coyote will walk in between and right into the traps.

Coyotes are skinned cased and the pelts are dried fur-side-out. Although it is a large animal, the coyote skins rather easily and peels clean. Since very little fat is left on the skin, the fleshing part of the operation is also easy. When the pelt is dry and ready for market, thoroughly comb and brush it. As the final part of the operation, fluff up the fur with brush strokes, from the tail toward the head.

Coyote trapping is never easy and it takes both time and practice to learn to make a good set. But after you get the hang of it and catch a few of these animals, you'll find that it isn't nearly as hard as you thought it would be.

11 | The Wolf

A full-grown timber wolf, the largest member of the canine family, is an awesome animal both in size and general appearance. Almost 3 feet tall at the shoulder, and often 6 feet or longer from the end of its nose to the tip of its tail, some prime specimens weigh in at close to 175 pounds. Just the thoughts of trapping one of these animals, or even meeting one face to face in the wilderness, is enough to make most trappers hang up their traps for good and take up some other occupation.

The timber wolf has a long-time reputation as a wanton destroyer of livestock, big-game animals, and even humans, with most of it undeserved. The animal's reputation does make interesting material for fictional books and magazine articles, however, and it is always one of the main subjects during yarn-spinning sessions around campfires at night in wolf country. These tales, dreamed up by trappers who had little else to do during the long winter months of isolation, have caused many a visiting fisherman to Canada's northern lakes to cast backward glances toward the shadows of the surrounding timber and crowd in a little closer to the fire.

Even though the timber wolf is a killer, most of its victims are waterfowl, Arctic hares, and lemmings. When it does turn to larger animals, these are usually the old, the sick, and the weak. Attacks on man just never happen. The wolf has an age-old fear

Ron Pittard

of man that won't let it get that close. Actually, the most danger-ous member of the canine family, and the one that has killed more humans than all the others combined, is man's best friend and family pet—good old faithful Rover.

Most trappers in the United States were born much too late to ever get a chance to match wits with the timber wolf. There are still a few left in the wilderness areas of Minnesota and Wiscon-sin, and maybe even a few in some of the northeastern states, but there's probably no more than fifty of these magnificent animals in all the contiguous states combined. And most of these carry sort of

112

a dual citizenship, and roam back and forth across the U.S.–Canadian border.

Within the last few years, wolf sightings have been reported in northern Washington, Idaho, Montana, and Yellowstone National Park, but there has been little physical evidence to back up these claims. One large wolflike animal was killed in Washington, but not even wildlife experts agree on exactly what it was. Most of the animals seen and reported as wolves were "supercoyotes" that had their fur all fluffed up for cold-weather insulation. These animals do look big when they are by themselves or with smaller coyotes, but when compared to a timber wolf, they could walk right under its belly.

Some areas in Alaska and Canada still have rather large populations of timber wolves. In some places, there are so many that reduction programs are being planned in order to protect the caribou and the moose. In certain areas the timber wolf has been overprotected; this has resulted in its overpopulation. And since they do have to eat something, and most of the smaller animals are gone, the wolves have turned to big-game animals in order to survive.

At one time several different members of the wolf family were found in most parts of the United States. The lobo, or buffalo, wolf roamed the central and southern plains and followed the buffalo herds. The white wolf lived in the more mountainous regions of Idaho, Washington, and Montana. There were also the prairie wolf, or coyote, the red wolf of Texas, the black wolf, found in the eastern part of the country, and the brush wolf that lived in the northern timbered regions of Minnesota and Wisconsin. Of all of these, the coyote and the brush wolf are all that remain in sufficient numbers to allow any trapping at all. A few dozen red wolves still remain in Texas, but these are classed as an endangered species.

Like the grizzly bear, the big wolves are wilderness animals. As the wilderness keeps on shrinking, the only wolf that has been able to adapt to the drastic change has been the coyote. With the red wolf almost gone, the brush wolf will be the next to go. And the mournful old wolf song, which was guaranteed to send a chill up the spine of every outdoorsman, will be gone forever and will be replaced by the insane, cackling yip of the coyote.

Most of the wolf trapping that is done in Alaska and Canada takes place in the subzero temperatures and deep snow of winter because this is the time when these animals are hungry and most readily come to bait. Hunger causes the wolf to forget some of its suspiciousness and to take chances that it wouldn't take otherwise. Strong, heavy snares are used in the established trails and extra-large steel traps are used near the sets.

BURIED BAIT SET   This set takes advantage of the habit of all members of the canine family of burying surplus food, with the intention of coming back to dig it up later. It is similar to the Dirt Hole Set made for coyotes and foxes, with the main difference being that the bait is buried in the snow, and one or two large traps, similar in size to the No. 4½ Newhouse, are placed directly on top of the bait and then covered with about 1 inch of powdered snow. A few drops of wolf scent are sprinkled on top of the traps to mark the location; then a few drops of raw wolf urine are sprinkled on a nearby tree or bush. When the wolf attempts to dig up the bait, it digs straight into the traps. Since the wolf is a large, strong animal, and hard to hold, it is most important that you wire all trap chains securely.

WOLF KILL OR LARGE BAIT SET   This set is made near the remains of a large animal that the wolves have been feeding on. Snares are hung in all the trails leading to the area, and then scent sets, similar to the Scent Post Set for coyotes, are made in a

40- or 50-foot radius of the bait. Sprinkle a few drops of raw wolf urine on a small tree or rock, and place two large traps approximately 16 inches in front of it.

I have never trapped a wolf, and never intend to, and thus have very little firsthand knowledge of methods used to trap this animal. However, I do know some Canadian trappers who are real experts. One of them uses a successful set that is quite a bit different. Wolves are cannibals, and seem to prefer the flesh of their own species over that of many other animals. This friend uses skinned-out wolf carcasses for bait, wires them to a tree, builds a brush cubby over and around them, and then places large traps in the entrance. This must work, because he always has several large wolf pelts by the end of the season.

Wolves are skinned cased. And since they are long, lanky animals and have little fat on their bodies, fleshing the pelt creates no problem. The pelts are dried fur-side-out, on stretchers similar in shape to that of the coyote stretcher, but twice as large. Take special care of these pelts because they represent a lot of money.

12 | The Bobcat

The bobcat is one of nature's most perfect predators. Equipped with night vision that rivals that of the horned owl, retractable, razor-sharp claws, and a set of sharp teeth to match, this 25- to 35-pound member of the cat family can easily catch, pull down, and kill any animal as large as a sheep, antelope, or small deer. The bobcat is rather short-winded and depends on patience and stealth to get it in close to its prey. When it gets into position, it comes unwound like a coiled spring, and not even a jackrabbit can equal its speed in a 50-yard dash.

All cats are meat eaters. Although they prefer to make their own kills and eat it while it is still fresh and bloody, they will feed on any reasonably fresh dead animal they happen to find. If you make a set where they can locate it, and if you use large baits, you can be fairly certain that they will readily come to the set.

Bobcats are found in almost every section of the United States, and vary in size, shape, color, and even local name depending on their geographical location. Called wildcat, bay lynx, red lynx, and lynx cat, the bobcat is a close relative of the larger Canada lynx that lives in the northern forests. All are closely related to the house cat. If you want to study behavior and habits that apply to all members of the feline clan, the household, hearthside "Tabby" is a very good place to start.

116

Ron Pittard

Like all wild animals, bobcats are creatures of habit, and they can be expected to do many things that other animals do. Unlike many of the other predators, however, cats kill strictly for food instead of for fun. If they make a kill on a large animal, they will cover it up with leaves and branches and return at regular intervals to feed on it until it is all eaten up. Rabbits, birds, reptiles, muskrats, nutria, and beaver make up most of the bobcat's diet, but if the winter is bad and food is scarce, it will turn to big-game

117

animals and domestic livestock. But with the exceptions of wounded or weak game animals, these occasions are rare.

In most areas bobcats breed in the early spring and from two to five kittens are born in June. They den in holes in rock ledges, in hollow trees, and in abandoned badger and coyote burrows. The mother takes care of the young, whereas the male seems to have

Cottontails are among the bobcat's favorite food items.

few family responsibilities. In fact, after the kittens are born, prowling males in the area become a liability to kitten survival. Because of some strange plan of nature, these old toms are cannibals, and kill and eat every male kitten they can find.

This habit of the old males, in eliminating future competition for the favors of the females in the area, seems to hold true for all members of the cat family, including the domestic cat. It reduces the annual population increase by at least 50 percent. This self-predation isn't as cruel as it may appear; it is the very thing that keeps their numbers well within the available food supply in the area, and keeps them disease free, healthy, and strong.

All North American cats are wilderness animals, and avoid close contact with man in every way possible. And regardless of whether it is the lynx of the north, the medium-size lynx cat of the high plains or western mountains, the smaller bobcat of the southern or central states, or the red cats found along the West Coast, all have similar habits. About the most difficult thing in trapping these animals is in finding them to start with. Many people spend their entire lifetime in good cat country but still never see one. Unless there happens to be a few inches of snow on the ground so you can see the tracks, there can be many cats in the area and you would never know it.

Cat action is always predictable because the cat's hunting habits form a definite pattern. You can almost always tell what the cat will eventually do, and part of the fun of cat trapping is in the suspense of waiting for the old cat to make up its mind to do it. Patience is the name of the game when it comes to trapping these animals. You may know that there are a number of cats in the area, and still not catch one for a week or more. And then all at once, for some inexplicable reason, every cat in the area will suddenly decide to visit your sets.

The old tom cats are solitary animals, and with the exception of the spring breeding season always hunt and travel alone. The female is usually accompanied by two or three kittens up until the time they pair off during the spring breeding season. All bobcats are prowling animals and they cover a lot of territory on a regular circuit. Regardless of the food available, they never seem to spend more than a few days in any one area before they get restless and move on. But veteran cat trappers know that these cats will always return at more or less regular intervals. Part of the secret to success is to have the sets ready and waiting.

The bobcat is one of the most inquisitive animals in the entire world, and this one trait has gotten more bobcats in serious trouble than all of their other habits combined. If it happens to run across anything unusual during its nightly travels, such as a hole that might have a rabbit in it, a place where a careless camper has dumped some litter, or even a fence post that might have a shiny tin can on top, the bobcat will stop and sometimes spend hours trying to figure out the what and why of it. And like its smaller cousin, the house cat, the bobcat is thoroughly fascinated by almost every object in motion.

Cats hunt by sight and nature has equipped the cat with night vision that allows it to detect the slightest movement. It seems to use this sense much more than it does its sense of smell when it hunts for food. I have never had much success in using scent in order to draw a bobcat to a set. There have even been times, when fresh tracks in the snow showed that an old cat had walked right by one of my sets and never even broke its stride, when I was willing to bet that a bobcat couldn't smell anything. But it can; it actually has a very good sense of smell—if and when this independent character takes a notion to use it.

At times, the odor of fresh beaver castor will call a cat in from quite a distance. The odor of catnip will hold it near a set after it gets there, and female cat urine, used during the spring breeding season, is a powerful attraction to every prowling tom in the area.

As far as traps and sets are concerned, the average bobcat is not too smart. Instead of being suspicious of a set, like the fox or the coyote, the bobcat's curiosity causes it to be just the opposite. This makes the bobcat surprisingly easy to trap. There are exceptions, of course. Occasionally an old cat will really tear up a set, but the average cat will only scratch around a little, chew on a few roots or bushes, and then stretch out and take it easy.

BAITED CUBBY SET   This is an excellent set for all members of the cat family. And like all sets, this one should also be made in an area where cats are known to hunt and travel. In beaver country, every cat around checks ponds and lodges at regular intervals. They also hunt the edges of muskrat swamps, and along and just under the rims of rocky ledges, for cottontail rabbits and other small rodents. Such locations as these are good places to make your sets.

The larger body-grip killer traps work well when placed in the entrances to small cubbies. In larger ones such as the Pole Cubby,

Pole Cubby Set

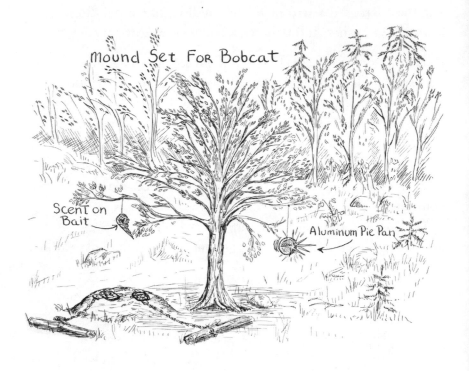

Mound Set For Bobcat

Scent on Bait

Aluminum Pie Pan

use either one or two No. 3 or No. 4 size steel traps, placed just inside the entrance. The traps can be placed on top of the ground and lightly covered with leaves, grass, or snow. Wire the traps solid because the trapped cat can put up quite a fight if it takes a notion to. Use a rather large bait, such as a rabbit, a skinned-out beaver, or muskrat carcass. Hang the bait up where the cat can easily see it. Tie it tight, so the cat can't grab it and pull it loose. Sprinkle a few drops of raw cat urine or catnip on a bush near the set. Do not sprinkle it on the traps, because if you do the cat will probably lie down, roll in it, and spring the traps and get away.

HANGING BAIT SET This is probably the best set for all cats; it not only draws hungry cats, but also those that are only curious.

122

No cat that finds it can resist checking it out thoroughly.

The ideal location for this set is in a tree near the center of a small clearing, or near any well-traveled trail. Hang a large bait, such as a rabbit, beaver, or muskrat carcass or dead chicken, from a limb where it can be seen from all directions. Hang this bait about 3 feet above the ground and use strong wire so the cat can't grab it and pull it down. Build a small mound from dirt or snow 6 to 8 inches high and 12 to 16 inches across, directly under the bait. Place two No. 3 or No. 4 size traps on top of the mound, and cover lightly. Stake the traps securely. For an added attraction, tie a small aluminum pie plate to a light string, and hang this from the tip of one of the outer limbs. Use cat scent, urine, or catnip at the base of the tree. When the cat sees the plate, twirling in the wind and flashing in the moonlight, it will come in close to investigate. It will locate the bait, use the mound for a handy step in order to reach it, and will step right into the trap.

Cats are skinned cased and stretched fur-side-out, and since they are large animals, it is usually best to hang them up to skin them. Cats peel easily but they do have a tender belly, so take extra care not to tear them. Cut the feet off, unless you have an exceptional pelt that might bring more money for a rug or taxidermy purposes. And if you think you do, contact the buyer before you skin it, because in most cases they prefer to do the skinning themselves.

Cats are naturally clean animals and have little fat on their bodies. This makes fleshing the pelt easy; what little there is to do can usually be done with a few strokes of the skinning knife. Pull the skin over the board fur-side-in. Let it dry for a day or so, and then turn it fur-side-out, slip it back on the board and hang it up to dry. Comb and brush it thoroughly before selling.

The most remarkable thing about the entire business of cat trapping has been the amazing rise in pelt prices within the last few years. Cats of the same quality caught and sold during the 1950s and 1960s for $8 to $10 each are now selling for as much as $400. The average lynx cat from Montana and Wyoming will probably bring a lucky trapper from $150 to $250 each.

Cat trapping has always been fun, but now it is a lot more fun—and much more rewarding.

13 | The Canada Lynx

There has always been considerable controversy about the relationship between the bobcat and the Canada lynx. Some believe that both of these animals are descendants of smaller European cats, and that climatic conditions and geographical locations account for the variations in color, size, and other characteristics. These animals do resemble each other in both looks and habit, and particularly so where their ranges overlap in the northern United States and southern Canada. But regardless of family origin, or its relationship to other members of the cat family, this whiskered old gentleman of the northern forests is the king of all the cats and is in a class all by himself.

The Canada lynx is a big animal, with an average weight of from 30 to 45 pounds. It is heavy bodied and has long legs and very big feet. The lynx also has large pointed ears with tufts of black hair extending out from the tips. It appears to be awkward, but don't let its looks deceive you. When danger or the sight of prey pulls its trigger, this big old cat can take off like a shot from a gun.

Like all members of the cat family, the lynx is a killer and won't hesitate in taking advantage of any big-game animal that is sick and weak. But since these are never too plentiful, most of the lynx's diet is made up of much smaller animals.

Ron Pittard

Unlike the bobcat that prefers more open country, the lynx likes the solitude of the deep northern forests. And since it has no liking for man or any of his improvements, it stays as far away from civilization as it possibly can. It will eat any kind of fresh meat that it happens to find, but seems to have a preference for the tender flesh of beaver. The lynx's winter fare includes tiny

126

squirrels, ptarmigan, Arctic hares, as well as the big-footed snow-shoe hare.

When the rabbit cycle is high and their food supply depend-able, the lynx population is also high. But when the rabbit popu-lation drops, as it seems to do every four or five years, the cat population quickly follows.

The lynx has little fear of man or traps but since its actions are rather unpredictable—it may make a lot of tracks in one area during the night, and be far away by morning—it takes a good trapper, one willing to put in long, cold hours at his job, to be successful in trapping these valuable animals. But if the lynx has found the hunting to be good in the area, and it is along the route of the animal's regular travels, it will usually return within a week

The lynx's winter food includes the snowshoe hare.

Ron Pittard

Snowshoe Trail Snare Set
For Lynx

or so. If your sets are ready and waiting, the chances for success are very good.

Like most wild animals, the lynx is also a creature of habit, and is very inquisitive. For example, the lynx will follow a snowmobile track or a trapper's snowshoe trail for miles. Taking advantage of this habit is one of the keys to trapping the lynx.

Since the lynx lives in cold country, there never have been many of these big cats in the United States. And while the lynx population is probably as large now as it ever was, their range has always been restricted to the deep snow and forests near our northern border. Both Alaska and Canada have healthy lynx populations. But like all cats, they control their own numbers and never seem to get thick in any area. Veteran lynx trappers con-

128

sider a single lynx in a square mile of frozen wilderness a veritable population explosion.

Snowshoe Trail Set   Because of the lynx's habit of following well-packed trails, this is one of the most popular sets for taking lynx. Moose and deer also follow these trails, and they have a habit of knocking down a well-placed snare before the lynx can get to it. In most areas it is necessary to place a barricade across the trail so the larger animals will either jump over or go around.

Snares have always been popular with wilderness trappers. They are light to carry and much cheaper than steel traps to buy, but many trappers find it still cheaper to buy a roll of wire and make their own. I wouldn't want to use one on an animal this large without a locking device, but these can be bought separate or even made at home by using a bent washer. Unlike steel traps that a few inches of new snow will put out of commission, the snare is hung up in the air, and unless freezing rain hits it, it is in place and ready to go. This trail set can be made with either snares or traps. If you do use traps, use No. 4 size, or larger, and wire them solid. Remember, the lynx has big snowshoe-type feet, and is a very strong animal.

The cubby set, similar to the one illustrated in the chapter on bobcats, is also an excellent set for lynx and can easily be made right along the snowshoe trail. Use large traps for this one, and set them back inside the entrance where they will have some protection from the snow.

Like the bobcat, the lynx knows where every beaver pond in the entire area is located, and even in the dead of winter, checks on these every time it gets a chance. Locations near the lodge or dam make good places for lynx sets, because the lynx that comes here are hungry and are looking for beaver to eat.

One of the best bait sets is very simple to make. Hang a skinned beaver carcass about 4 feet off the ground, and against the trunk of a large tree. Place two large traps under it, about 16 inches out from the base. Wire them solid and cover lightly with leaves or snow. When the cat locates the bait it will rear up on its hind feet, sink its front claws in the bait, and attempt to pull it down. When it does, those big rear feet will waltz right into the jaws of the trap.

Killer Trap Set   This is a set that has been developed since the efficient 330 Conibear killer trap came on the market, and it has quickly became the favorite of many Canadian lynx trappers. Tie a fresh beaver castor to the trigger of the 330 Conibear. Do this before setting the trap. Unless the guards are in place, attempt no adjustments because like any other large trap, this one is extremely dangerous.

Hang the trap against the trunk of a large tree, so that the bait is approximately 2 feet off the ground. When the cat reaches in with its teeth to get this tasty morsel and attempts to pull it away from the tree, this big killer trap goes off like a bomb and literally explodes. As the jaws start to spring, the backswing hits the tree, the trap violently jumps forward and catches the unfortunate old lynx right behind the ears. The impact alone usually breaks its neck, but if this doesn't quite do the job, it will only take a few minutes to finish it.

Since lynx sets are made in remote areas far from civilization, there are no problems with prowling domestic dogs with this set. But you should use caution near cross-country trails because sled dogs have been known to get in it.

The lynx is skinned cased and stretched fur-side-out. And the method used in processing its pelt is the same as that of the bobcat. Take extra care of this pelt, because not only is it big in size, but at the present time it also represents some mighty big money.

14 | The Foxes

Almost every trapper in the United States and Canada has some member of the fox family along his trapline. Their range is widespread, from Mexico in the south, to the floating ice in the northern Arctic regions. Members of this large family come in various sizes, shapes, and colors but all are similar in habits, and all bear a close relationship to the other North American canines, dogs, coyotes, and wolves.

Foxes are carnivorous, and they kill other animals in order to live. While several wolves can make short work of a caribou, and even under the right conditions, a big bull moose, the smaller cousin of the family, the fox, has to content itself with prey that it can handle. And this is seldom larger than some farmer's hen, a cottontail rabbit, grasshopper, or mouse.

All foxes hunt at night. However, in the dead of winter, when their food supply is short, foxes can be seen in the daytime, especially during the early morning and late evening hours. When you do see one in the daytime, you can be sure that there are at least a dozen more that are keeping out of sight.

In areas where the food supply is plentiful, all members of the fox clan are prolific. They breed in the early spring and usually have a litter of from four to ten young.

Fox dens are usually found in hollow logs, holes in the rocks, or the abandoned burrow of some larger animal. If they live in badger country, badger holes are the ones they usually choose. Young foxes are born blind, and they stay in the den until they are about a month old. As they grow older, they follow their parents during their nightly search for food. Both the male and the female take care of the family—the female provides the young with milk and protection, while the male hunts for fresh food and brings it home to the family.

Because of their small size, foxes have a number of natural enemies. The horned owl probably takes more small foxes than all the others. Eagles take medium-size foxes and have even been known to attack the adults. Where fox range overlaps that of the coyote, this animal will kill every fox that it can. Highways are death-traps for foxes because of their habit of feeding on road-killed animals. The automobile can probably be credited with more fox deaths than any other single cause, including the trapper. This may surprise you, but it is a fact of life.

Foxes have always been an important animal in the North American fur trade. Pelts from most foxes have a high market value, and are well worth the attention of any trapper. The fox is not as hard to trap as the coyote, and doesn't even begin to compare with a battle-scarred old beaver in open water. All foxes are exceptionally smart animals. Fox trapping, regardless of species, is a true battle of wits between man and animal, with most of the odds on the side of the animal. By a careful study of its habits, however, a trapper can learn to "outfox" it and cause it to make a foolish move. And when it does, his trap will be in the proper place to catch it.

Unless a trapper is willing to put in long hours of study, and then use every precaution when making his sets, he will have little chance of catching the fox. In trapping foxes, experience is the best teacher. Especially valuable is the experience that comes

132

in the form of a veteran fox trapper willing to take a youngster with him on his trapline and teach him a few tricks of the trade.

There are many members of the fox family in North America: the prairie swift or kit fox, the red fox, the cross fox, the gray fox, the silver gray fox, the blue fox, the white or Arctic fox, the black fox, the red-side gray fox, and probably others. Some of these are distinct and separate species, some are subspecies, and some are color phases of one species, and at times, even a mixture of two. Not even the naturalists and trained game biologists are in agreement about the classification of the various species and subspecies. I will leave the scientific arguments to those who qualify and will merely attempt to sort out the species and color phases that mean the most to the trapper.

The red fox has the widest range, the largest population, and is the most important fox to trappers. This 25-pound fox, with the red-orange coat, and white tip on its long, bushy tail, brings trappers millions of dollars each year. The best pelts come from Alaska and the states of North Dakota, Montana, Wisconsin, and Minnesota, with about the same size and fur quality coming from the adjoining Canadian provinces.

In general, the red fox has learned to live in close proximity with man, in cleared areas where mice, rabbits, ground-nesting birds, and small rodents are plentiful. In some areas this animal is a serious threat to game birds and is a barnyard nuisance second to none. Elsewhere, the red fox kills enough rats and mice to pay its way. In fact, a few red foxes are pretty good neighbors to have, and you should be grateful for their presence.

The gray fox is the southern member of the family. Slightly smaller than the red fox, with an average weight of from 12 to 15 pounds, this dark gray animal is found from coast to coast south of the Mason-Dixon line. Sometimes called the red-side gray,

Red fox.

from its color, and swamp fox, from its habit of seeking food in the marshes and along the edge of lakes and streams, the gray fox has most of the habits of all its northern cousins. It is a meat eater and a killer. It does most of its hunting and feeding at night, and in some areas it is a serious nuisance because of its habit of sneaking into the barnyard and helping itself to poultry.

The gray fox has a tail that looks too long for its body. When it is running all-out, it looks almost like it was pulling a trailer. Catlike in its actions, the gray fox will often climb a tree when pressed hard by hounds.

134

Because it lives in warmer regions, the pelt of the gray fox is never as valuable as that of the red. Nevertheless, due to the current high prices on all long-haired animals, the gray fox is well worth trapping. Study its habits, and get to know it before attempting to trap it.

The Arctic fox is pure white and is found only in the far north. White foxes live in the same general area as the black fox and the blue fox, and many northern trappers claim that they all are color phases of the same species, and that white, black, and blue pups are often found in the same litter. None of these northern foxes are found in the United States, with the exception of Alaska and some of the off-shore islands. They range from Alaska north,

Gray fox.

135

Arctic fox.

around the top of North America, and down into Manitoba on Hudson Bay. Occasionally, a few of these animals drift as far south as the Churchill River, in northern Saskatchewan.

Most Arctic foxes are found within a few miles of salt water where they hunt the ocean beaches for dead fish, shorebirds, and seals. During the long, cold winter months, when their food supply is short, some of the white foxes follow the polar bear on its travels out on the ice pack, and they feed on the remains of the seals it kills.

Because of the extremely cold climate where these animals live, their coats are long and silky, with thick underfur that often looks

136

woolly. The pelts of all the northern foxes are highly prized by the fur trade and bring fabulous prices. However, the pelts of the white fox stain easily, and very few perfect pelts ever reach the market.

Since these small northern foxes live in remote areas and have had little contact with civilization, they have never learned to fear man. This makes them easy to trap. In the dead of winter when their natural food supply is always short, they will readily come to any baited set. Most Arctic foxes are trapped on ocean beaches, in the deep snow, or on the ice. Since none of these conditions is ideal for the use of the steel trap, these animals are usually caught in snares, deadfalls, or crude cage-type box traps made of driftwood.

Similar methods are used for trapping red and gray foxes. Both are smart animals and extremely cautious. Foxes follow a definite pattern in their habits and as soon as a trapper learns this, it only takes a little imagination on his part to devise different methods of making sets that will trap them. They always hunt in the same general area and follow the same trails. They have both day and night vision, a good sense of smell, and are always inquisitive with regard to food or the presence of a female of the species. But trappers have a habit of following patterns, too—especially by making too many of the same kind of sets along their traplines—and it won't take an animal as smart as a fox long to learn to avoid them completely.

Dirt Hole Set   Before the ground freezes hard this is one of the best fox sets. Similar to the one illustrated in the chapter on coyotes, but with some differences in bait, scent, and location, this set will draw every fox in the immediate area. If it looks natural, and everything happens to work right, trapping the animal with this set will be no problem at all.

137

Log Crossing Set

Foxes are small animals and a No. 1½ size trap will easily hold one. Since with the Dirt Hole Set the jaws of the trap have to rise through a layer of dirt, I suggest the use of No. 2 or No. 3 size traps. Long-spring traps might be a little bit stronger, but under-spring or jump traps are the easiest to conceal.

Dig the hole at the base of a small rock or bush that the animal can easily see over, and spread the dirt in a fan-shaped pattern. Use a liquid or chunk bait in the hole, and place two traps about 12 inches in front of it. Bury the traps so the pans lay just below ground level, and dig the trap bed large enough so that you can place a stake or grapnel directly under it. Use a trap-pan cover, and cover the trap with approximately ¼ inch of sifted dirt. Use a good call lure near this set. One with a faint skunk odor in

138

it reaches out and works wonders on a fox. During the late winter or early spring, sprinkle a few drops of female fox urine on a nearby bush.

LOG CROSSING SET   Any trapper lucky enough to have a few old stream-crossing logs along his line has a ready-made setup for adding some extra dollars to his trapline income. All veteran trappers know this and use these logs to a good advantage, but many younger and inexperienced trappers pass them by. When they do, they are passing up one of the best chances they ever had to trap foxes and other wild members of the canine family.

All cats, coyotes, and foxes are travelers. These animals are also good swimmers, and will quickly take to the water if forced to do so, but they prefer to keep their feet dry. They will even go a mile

Conibear Trap Set For Fox

or so out of their way to use a log to cross a stream. The wiser and more wary animals prefer to cross on a narrow log, instead of a wide one or even a man-made bridge. Some animals, especially foxes, use these logs as a place to play. While they are running back and forth above the water, and have their minds on keeping their balance, it's never too much of a problem to arrange for them to stick their heads into the noose of a snare or to step on the pan of a well-concealed trap. If the laws of your state allow snares to be used, this log is probably the best location that you will ever find for them. You may have to wire or nail a small branch on each side to hold the noose in place, but this will take only a few minutes, and it should result in one of the most productive sets along the entire trapline.

Unless you happen to have an old rotten, moss-covered log, a steel trap may be hard to conceal. If it is, the best place for the trap is on the bank, and in the position where the animal will jump off the log and directly into the open jaws of the trap. Use a No. 2 or No. 3 size trap. Bury the trap similar to other sets for wary animals, and wire it securely.

If you decide that the trap would be best on the log, chop a notch to the proper size and depth. Rub in mud to disguise the fresh cut. Place the trap in position, fill around it, and cover lightly with moss and damp leaves. Place a fist-size stone on either side of the trap, and space these so that the animal will step over the stone and into the jaws of the trap.

If this set is in an area where these fur-bearers vary in size, use either a No. 3 or No. 4 size trap on the log. Wire the trap to the log, and allow enough free chain and wire so that the trapped animal will jump into the water and quickly drown.

Do not make this set in waterfowl or coon-hunting country. It is better not to make it at all than to take a chance on costing a fellow outdoorsman a valuable dog. Use no scent near this set.

FENCE CROSSING SET   Like all members of the canine family, the fox is a hunter and does a lot of traveling in search of its prey. In most good fox country, deep snows at higher elevations drive the small animals and birds into the valleys, valleys mean farms, and farms mean woven-wire fences. Where a fox trail goes through, or under, a fence is a perfect location to make a set. Since this set is usually made in the snow and a steel trap might not work, because of new snow or freezing conditions, use either a light snare or one of the larger body-grip killer traps.

CAMPFIRE SET   Members of the canine family like to explore abandoned camp sites, and to dig into the ashes of a cold campfire for any bit of food that might remain. They expect to find human odor at these locations, so you don't have to be as careful here as you do when making the other sets for foxes.

You can make your own campfire if you wish, but for best results use an established campground, after the camping season is over. Every fox in the area knows where these are located and visits them every time it gets a chance. Many experienced trappers bait these several times with bits of cheese, bacon rind, and lard crackling, well in advance of the opening of the trapping season.

Dig a hole in the ashes, approximately 4 inches deep and 16 inches across. Place the surplus ashes on a piece of canvas. Put the stake or grapnel in the hole, and put two traps, size No. 2 or No. 3, directly on top. Use a trap-pan cover, and sift approximately ¼ inch of light ashes over the traps. Burn a small amount of dry grass directly over the traps, and when you have a small blaze going, drop in a few pieces of bacon rind, meat scraps, or lard cracklings. For additional drawing power, a few burned chicken feathers seems to work wonders. Be sure not to use any sticks or bones that might interfere with the action of the trap.

141

Scatter the extra ashes that you have on the canvas, and use a dash of fox call lure on a nearby tree. Place this lure several feet above the ground, so that the odor can drift over a wide area.

This is a simple set and easy to make. Even an inexperienced youngster can catch fox in this one.

The fox is one of the easiest of all animals to skin and stretch, but millions of dollars are lost each year through sloppy skinning and poor pelt handling procedures. It seems a real shame that any trapper would go to all the time and trouble it takes to learn to catch this wary, valuable animal, and still not be willing to put out just a little extra time and effort in order to take proper care of its pelt. These are the same trappers that constantly complain

142

Bait Staked Out in
Water 6 to 8 Inches Deep

Call Lure on Bank

Water Set For Fox

about poor fur prices, and blame the fur buyer and the market in general—everyone but themselves.

Not too long ago, I visited one of the nation's leading fur auctions, and while there I got the opportunity to run my fingers through the fur of some top-quality pelts that were shipped in from all sections of Canada and the United States, including Alaska. I also got to see many pelts that were top quality when the fox wore them, but were ruined and wasted when these beautiful pelts fell into the hands of some slob trapper.

Some were stretched open, others dried fur-side-in, and others had their bellies torn open and no attempt had been made at sewing the damage. Some had their tails pulled completely off, while others were still covered with dried blood and were badly stained. After I got a good look at these, I reached the conclusion that many trappers must have more money than I do, and can afford to take less than half price for their pelts.

Fur prices are good, but only for well-handled pelts. Regardless of whether a pelt came off a raccoon, a mink, or a beautiful red fox, the trapper who has the knowledge and ability to take care of it properly will always be the trapper who brings home the most money. Fur buyers want these pelts because they help him sell a lot of the poor ones, and most buyers will pay a little bonus in order to get them.

The first thing I do after I take a fox out of the trap is to drop it into a large plastic bag and give it a healthy blast or two from a can of insect spray. Then I tie the top and leave it tied until I get home from tending my trapline. This is the only way I have found to get rid of the fleas and other crawling vermin that try to find a new home on the trapper, after the body of the fox starts to get cold. These might not bother some fox trappers, but they make me mighty nervous.

The fox is an easy animal to skin, and you use the same method that you do with any other animal that you want to stretch cased. The only trouble spots I have ever encountered when taking care of this animal are the tender flanks and belly and the tip of the tail. If you take special care of these places, you will have no problems with the rest of the animal. Use a tail stripper to separate the skin on the tail from the bone, and then use a sharp-pointed knife to rip it clear to the end.

After the skinning is completed, the fleshing is easy and can usually be done right on the fur stretcher. Scrape off what little fat there is and wipe off excess grease with a dry rag. Stitch the tips of the top and bottom lips together. This makes the pelt look better, and is one of those extra touches that never fails to catch the eye of the buyer. Wipe off all blood, because fox fur is easily stained. Pick out the burrs that will come out easy, but if they are

144

matted and fur pulls with them, leave them in. The fur dresser can take care of them later. Pull the pelt on the board fur-side-in. Check it the next day and then turn it fur-side-out, and hang it up to dry.

It will probably take an extra thirty minutes to do a good job on a fox pelt. But after you brush and comb it until it glistens, you can be assured of a premium price, and the extra $5 or $10 that you get from your work will usually come in handy.

15 | The Badger

The badger, a 25- to 30-pound member of the weasel family, is found in most areas of the United States and southern Canada, with the highest populations centered in the high plains and drier regions of both countries. For some unknown reasons, badgers never seem to be too plentiful. And no one that I know has ever made a lot of money trapping them, but a good working knowledge of how to trap them can always mean some extra money for the fox or coyote trapper. Usually, if you will agree to trap badger from a rancher's land, he will be more receptive to the idea of your trapping the other fur-bearers on his land as well.

Livestock ranchers hate the badger because of its habit of digging holes in its search for food, with each of these 6- to 8-inch holes becoming an open trap for a valuable horse or cow to step in. Worse yet, if a running horse with a rider happens to hit one of these holes at high speed, the result is almost always broken bones and possibly even death for man or animal.

Aside from this, the mounds of dirt thrown up from each of these digging operations means the loss of valuable top soil and grass because the badger digs up the clay and gravel from underground and spreads it out on top. Although the loss of approximately a square yard of grass to each mound usually means very little to a western rancher, when you multiply this damage by a

thousand, and in many cases even ten thousand, in several square miles of range land, this begins to add up into acres, and also into the loss of thousands of dollars that very few people can spare. Even though the badger is providing the landowner with a valuable service in ridding his property of range-land pests—each hole that the badger digs always has a nest of ground squirrels, moles, prairie dogs, or gophers at the lower end of it—the cure is always much worse than the original problem, and it leaves the land in such a mess that it will take it many years to recover.

The badger is a rough, rugged character when it comes to a

fight. It is mild-mannered and never seems to go out of its way to look for trouble, but its short, stubby legs and long, sharp claws and teeth were made for digging and fighting, instead of running. And while it may look like a pushover to a young, eager bobcat, coyote, or dog, the older animals have learned from experience that the badger is one animal to leave strictly alone. If some young predator does happen to grab it, it won't take the old badger over a few seconds to give him an education.

Until the last few years most badgers were caught by accident in traps set for coyotes and foxes. But now, a prime badger pelt, with good underfur, is worth almost as much as a coyote pelt. For the first time, badger trapping is a paying proposition. The badger is not a hard animal to trap, but you do have to learn its habits. And the more you know about this animal, the better chance you have for success.

The badger is a nocturnal animal and does most of its hunting at night. Like all members of the large weasel family, it is a killer and will eat almost any kind of reasonably fresh meat that it can find—a variety of ground nesting birds, rabbits, roots, insects, and small burrowing rodents. It has a keen sense of smell and will come to any kind of scent that arouses its curiosity or that it can associate with food.

A common mistake many inexperienced trappers make is setting the trap in the entrance of a fresh-dug hole, because chances are the badger has already dug out some small burrowing rodent and is gone. These holes are not dens. Even if the badger is in the hole when you make the set, its habit of bulldozing a wave of dirt ahead of it, as it comes out of the hole, will almost always cover up or spring the trap.

DIRT HOLE SET   Similar to the one used for coyotes and foxes, this is an excellent set for badger. Use at least two No. 2 or No. 3

size traps. Set them 6 to 8 inches in front of the hole, and also about the same distance apart. The badger is built like a large shoe box, with a short leg on each corner. Since its usual action is to walk straight into a set, take the bait, and then back straight out, it will usually straddle a single trap. If the animal does happen to throw the trap, it will be because it laid down on the trap, and hit the pan with its chest.

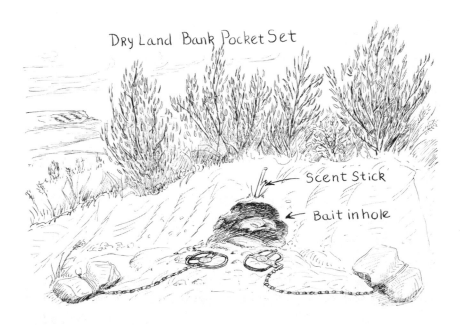

Dry Land Bank Pocket Set

Scent Stick

Bait in hole

Bury the traps in the usual manner. Use the trap-pan cover, and cover the trap with about ¼ inch of fine sifted dirt. Stake all badger traps solid. If you don't, the badger will either find a hole to crawl in or will dig one of its own, and you will have to do some digging of your own to get the trapped animal out.

DRY LAND BANK POCKET SET This is my favorite trap for badgers. Set it along the edge of a dry wash or a ditch bank in an area

149

where badger sign is plentiful. If possible, locate an old, abandoned hole about the right size, or find a location near a well-traveled trail, and dig a hole of your own about 16 inches deep and 12 inches wide—and high—at the front. Use a rabbit, bird, or skinned muskrat carcass for bait, in the rear of the hole, and pin it in place with a sharp stick.

Use two large traps and space them similar to those in the Dirt Hole Set. Cover them thoroughly and you'll also have a good chance at catching a prowling bobcat, fox, or coyote. Use several drops of scent near the entrance—almost anything with an intense, lingering odor will do—and be sure that you use a strong wire and stake the trap tight. Use a metal stake at least 16 inches long, because every badger you trap will do a lot of chewing and digging.

WINTER DEN SET   The badger semihibernates in winter. It usually stores up some food, and it is not unusual for the animal to stay in its den for at least a month during the dead of winter. However, a few sunshiny days in a row will usually bring it out. It will prowl around, even in the snow, and the fresh tracks that it makes will lead a trapper right back to its den. This den looks similar to those that it makes when digging for prey, but the entrance is always worn and has tracks leading in both directions. Even when the mound is snow covered, you can tell if the badger is inside by frozen vapor in the entrance, and by an air hole.

This set is an excellent place for one of the larger body-grip killer traps. Place sticks or grass under the jaws so it won't freeze down, and lay it flat over the hole. When the badger starts out, and attempts to squeeze through it, it will snap shut and grab the animal by the neck or the body.

Badger pelts are easy to take care of because the skin is loose and easy to peel, there's only a short stub of a tail to worry about, and not much fat on the body. This animal is skinned open and stretched flat, to the general shape of the animal.

Due to its digging habits, occasionally the badger is covered with mud when you take it out of the trap. If so, wash the animal off with cool water before you skin it. Then, before stretching, hang the pelt up until the fur is completely dry. Tack it to a square of plywood, a wood frame, or even to the inside of the barn door; it really doesn't matter where you hang it so long as it is in a place where the air is dry.

The badger pelt is one that you might be able to sell to a taxidermist for rug-making purposes; this usually means a bonus of a few extra dollars. Check with him before skinning because if he does buy it, he will want the feet and the claws left on, and probably will want to do the skinning himself. When skinning for the regular fur market, cut the feet off, but save the long claws from the front feet. You might want to use them yourself, or sell them to someone else, for making a "bear claw necklace."

Badger fur is used for making streamer fishing flies, fine artist's brushes, and trim on luxurious ladies' garments.

16 | The Wolverine

Probably more fiction has been written about the wolverine than any other fur-bearing animal. Most of these tales have one thing in common: the writers were more interested in knocking out a real north-country thriller than they were in sticking to facts. As a result, many people believe the wolverine to be some kind of an evil genius, with uncanny abilities that no animal could possibly have in reality.

These tales were started by superstitious natives in the far north who believed in animal gods, ghosts, and many kinds of devils. When they ran across something they couldn't quite understand or cope with, it was a lot easier to blame it on the supernatural than it was to spend the time and trouble trying to solve their problems. As these campfire tales spread to the saloons where prospectors, hunters, and writers heard them, they quickly grew with the telling, and before too much time had passed the wolverine had gained a reputation it really didn't deserve.

Mother Nature must have had an off day when she put the wolverine together, because this animal seems to be made up of a rather misfit collection of cast-off or leftover parts from other animals. Take the ears of a raccoon, the head of a small dog, the wits of a fox, the feet of a bear, the legs of a badger, the heart of a lion, the musk glands of a skunk, the evil temper of a hornet, the

152

appetite of a garbage disposal unit, the hoarding habits of a mountain pack rat, and then combine all these dubious features into the 30-pound body of a dark brown member of the weasel family and you just naturally come up with a frustrated bundle of trouble. And then, to top it all off, you place this critter in the deep snow of the cold country, where the easiest path to a full belly is right down the snowshoe trail of a hard-working trapper, and you are bound to wind up with lots of problems and a trapline nuisance that is second to none.

The wolverine is a wilderness animal, and is the largest and most powerful member of the weasel family. It lives in the dense forests of Alaska, Canada, and in some of the colder regions of the United States. Wolverine fur is extremely valuable and well worth the time it takes to trap this animal. At the present time, a prime wolverine pelt will bring a trapper between $100 and $200. Most trappers will put up with a few inconveniences for a chance at that kind of money.

The wolverine is a nocturnal animal that will eat almost anything when it is really hungry. Its usual fare consists of rabbits, fish, berries, squirrels, marmots, and mice. It could easily handle a caribou or moose fawn or even an old caribou or moose that was sick and weak. Like all weasels, the wolverine is a killer and seems to enjoy its bloody trade, but since it is always hungry very little of its prey ever goes to waste.

Called the "glutton, skunk bear, Indian devil," and other names not even that nice, the wolverine follows lynx, bears, and wolves and takes over their kills. All of these predators are much larger and stronger, but this brown bundle of fury can hold its own with the best of them. And if bluffing and fighting isn't enough to run them off, the wolverine can emit a strong, foul-smelling, skunklike odor that no other animal can stand to be around. They will gag and roll in the snow—and the battle is quickly over!

The wolverine is constantly prowling for food. It will wreck every set and every fur and food cache or trapper's cabin that it can claw into. After one or more of these animals find a trapline and start their free-loading rampage, the only way to stop them is to kill them—and that isn't always as easy as it sounds.

The wolverine is on the same mental level as the average red fox, and regardless of what you have been led to believe, it is no magician when it comes to avoiding traps. However, it is a strong animal that has no trouble pulling out of the small traps set for marten or mink. This has contributed to the wolverine's reputa-

Staples

Nails To
hold Peg

Trigger

Snare Loop

Single Loop OF
wire around Peg

Snowshoe Trail Snare Set
For Wolverine

Baited Tree Set

tion of being almost impossible to trap and hold. But if you catch it in a set made for a lynx or a wolf, or make a special set for it, these traps will hold it without any problem at all. And when they do, another part of the myth and mystery that surrounds the wolverine quickly vanishes.

One efficient all-weather set for the wolverine is a snare hung in the snowshoe trail, similar to the set made for the wolf and the lynx. But since the wolverine has strong jaws and sharp, bone-crushing teeth, it will usually chew its way out of a snare in a hurry unless some method is used to jerk it off its feet. Veteran wolverine trappers use a trigger arrangement and anchor their snares to a sack of rocks or a log that will fall. This ensures that the set will spring, even when the temperature drops to 30 or 40 degrees below zero.

Another good set for the wolverine is the baited cubby. Use a skinned beaver carcass, a moose head, or even a rabbit and wire the bait firmly to a tree before building the cubby around it. If you want to make this set exclusive for wolverine, rub the foul-smelling musk from this animal on the bait; this will keep all the other animals away. This is a good set to use on one of the larger body-grip killer traps. If steel traps are used, choose No. 4 size, or larger. Use two traps and tie the trap chains in opposite directions so the traps will be separated by at least 12 inches. When the animal is caught in one, it will usually step right into the other. Bury the traps until the pans set level with the ground. Use a pan cover, and then conceal the traps with evergreen needles or small leaves. When trapping in snow, use waxed paper under the trap to keep the frost from coming up. Use this also for a pan cover, and then dust over with powdered snow. This set will take lynx, wolf, fox, fisher, and marten, if it is made in an area where these animals live. Use extreme care when making it, because all of these are valuable animals.

Wolverine pelts are usually skinned open and stretched flat, but since some fur buyers prefer to have them cased, it's a good idea to check with the buyer in advance to find out how he wants them. This animal is in high demand by the taxidermists, who will usually pay above regular pelt prices if you happen to have an animal of exceptional size and fur quality. So check with them also before you start the skinning.

Like most weasels, very few wolverines are fat, so fleshing the pelt is easy. All that is usually required is a little scraping around the edge of the pelt with a dull knife. Tack the pelt to a frame or a square of plywood and put it in a well-ventilated place to dry.

For some reason, both the population and the range of the wolverine are increasing and shifting to the south. Within the last few years, sightings of this animal have even been reported in California, Utah, and Colorado. If some animal starts robbing your trapline and it leaves a track like a cub bear, you had better get out some big traps; chances are good that a wolverine has moved into your area.

17 | The Otter

Not too many years ago, the otter's range covered most of the watered areas on the North American Continent. A thriving number of these animals were almost always found in any natural lake or stream that had a dependable supply of fish and other food. But the otter is a shy animal, and when man and his bulldozers move in, the otter has to move out. Now, in the United States at least, much of the otter's natural habitat has diminished almost to the vanishing point, and its population also has dropped.

The otter is a large animal, many times larger than its cousin, the mink, whom it resembles in other ways. An average-size male otter will usually weigh between 20 and 25 pounds, and will measure about 4½ feet long, from the end of its nose to the tip of its tail.

The otter is awkward on land but is as graceful as a seal in the water. Most of its diet is made up of fish, snails, crawfish, frogs, and turtles; but if these happen to be in short supply, or if it wants a change of fare, it will also kill and eat muskrats, ducks, and other waterfowl. And since the otter is a weasel, with the killer instinct of all the other members of this blood-thirsty clan, it sometimes makes a game of killing.

Naturalists believe there are as many as twenty separate species of otter scattered around the world, but North America has

Ron Pittard

only one species. Apparently, geographical differences account for the variation in size, pelt quality, and color of these fur-bearing animals. The fur trade recognizes four different classifications: the smaller southern otter, the northern otter, the Pacific Coast otter, and the Alaskan otter. Regardless of where they are found, from the swamps of Florida and Louisiana to the streams and lakes of Alaska and northern Canada, they all have the same general habits, they eat more or less the same food, and the methods used to trap them are generally the same.

Like other members of the weasel family, the male otter is a restless traveler and does most of his traveling alone. The female

160

confines her ramblings to a much smaller area and is usually accompanied by several kittens from her early spring litter. Otters make a lot of tracks and cover a lot of territory, but their feeding and traveling habits form a definite pattern. When you find otter sign in an area, you can almost always depend on the animal to return to the same place within one or two weeks; and you can have your sets waiting and ready to catch it.

TV and movies have shown the otter to be docile and gentle. Don't be misled—this is not the true nature of any member of the weasel family. These films were taken of otters that have spent their entire lives in captivity, and the otter that the trapper has to deal with is a completely different animal. It may appear to be playful, and like to slide down slick banks and splash in the water, but these habits have nothing to do with a gentle disposition. While the average otter is not aggressive toward larger animals, it is a short-tempered killer when seeking prey, or in defense of its life. And it is one of the few animals that can stand up and do battle with a Canada lynx or a wolverine, and have a good chance of winning the battle.

The otter is a creature of habit. Although it is a strong swimmer and is as agile as a trout in the water, it does a lot of its traveling along the bank. It has a habit of taking shortcuts across oxbows in a stream and also from one body of water to another near by. Tracks will show these otter trails, especially when they are made in soft sand or fresh snow. These are the places that veteran otter trappers look for to make their sets.

The otter has a keen sense of smell and is very inquisitive. Its curiosity will often cause it to approach a set that is baited with fresh fish. They might not eat the bait, but if a good otter gland lure is used in connection with the set, every otter that happens by will come in close to look it over.

The otter's ability to avoid traps is highly overrated. In my opinion, as well as that of other trappers, the average otter is no harder to trap than the average mink. The otter is a much larger and stronger animal—a regular demon when caught in a trap—so it is hard to hold, but large killer traps, steel traps, or snares set in the right locations will allow the average trapper to catch and hold the otter with little trouble.

Moss-covered floating logs, especially those with one end anchored to the bank, are prime locations for making otter sets. For most sets, two traps, No. 3 or larger, are much better than one. If at all possible, keep the traps under 3 or 4 inches of water, and covered with mud or leaves. Stagger the traps on both sides of the trail traveled by the animal. Use the one-way slide on the wire for drowning. If the water is too shallow for this, be sure and anchor

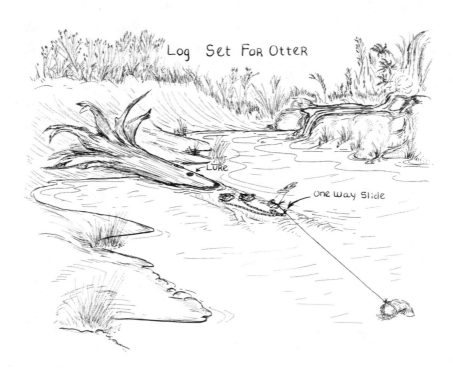

Log Set For Otter

Lure

One Way Slide

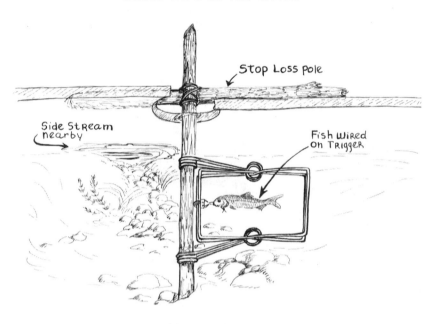

UndeR Ice Set FoR OtteR

Stop Loss pole

Side StReam nearby

Fish wiRed on TRiggeR

the traps in the water so the trapped animal cannot reach the log or the bank.

BANK POCKET SET Use two traps for this; keep the traps under water and fasten them to a drowning wire, with one-way slide. Weight the wire with a sack of rocks or gravel, weighing at least 30 pounds, and put it in at least 3 feet of water. Use fish for bait, and place a few drops of otter lure near the entrance to the set.

Otter slides are easy to find, but they are difficult places to make a set with a conventional trap. The animal is moving fast when it hits the water and usually has its front feet folded tight against its chest; this leaves a very small target for a trap to get hold of. But some of these slides are perfect locations for one of the larger body-grip killer traps.

163

Runway Set For Otter

Place Stick or Pole over set

Some of the old-style Newhouse traps, with the raised pan and long teeth in the jaws, are still used by some trappers in otter slides. These work reasonably well, but they catch the animal by the front leg or chest and punch a lot of holes in a valuable pelt. Other sets are just as good and do less damage. Northern trappers still use snares at otter slides, and attach them to a drowning wire or pole, or a spring pole that will lift the snared animal clear out of the water.

SIDE STREAM SET   This set is similar to the one illustrated in the chapter for mink, and is a good set for the otter. Locate a place where a small side enters the main stream and place one of the large killer traps right in the entrance. Cover the top and sides with brush and weeds to break up the outline. About 10 feet up the small stream, use a few drops of otter lure on a stone or a bush.

164

BEAVER DAM SET   This is an excellent set for otter; it catches the large males that do a lot of traveling. All beaver dams have a spillway, and these are regular highways for every otter that travels the stream. Use a large killer trap at the lower end of the spillway, and break up the outlines with brush. If the channel is deep enough, place the trap under water, and place sticks or a small log on top so the animal will dive and attempt to go through the trap. This also makes a very good set for beaver.

All otter are skinned cased. Since there is little fat on the animal, fleshing the pelt poses no problem. Before you pull the pelt on the board to stretch it, check with your buyer to see which way he wants the fur turned. Alaskan otter has always been turned fur-side-out, but the accepted custom in the lower forty-eight states has been to turn it fur-side-in. Some buyers want the pelts one way, others another. They are the people who put up the money, and it is usually worth a few extra dollars if you turn these pelts the way they want them.

18 | The Marten

Not too many years ago, the marten was one of North America's most valuable fur-bearers. Called American sable by the fur trade, the glossy, brown pelt of this animal quite often brought a hard-working trapper as much as $75 or $80. Present pelt prices are somewhat lower, but they are on the increase. Any trapper who can spend a few weeks in the rugged backcountry, where most of these animals live, can be assured of an outstanding trap-line adventure, and a chance to make some pretty good money as well. You couldn't hope for a better combination than that!

The marten is a tree-climbing member of the weasel family. Larger and with longer legs than the mink, the marten acts and even sounds like a cat. In general body shape and features, how-ever, it looks like a tiny brown fox that would weigh from 3 to 5 pounds. Most martens have long, silky fur of deep chocolate brown, with a prominent orange or white patch under their chins. Fur quality depends on the climate where these animals live. The best pelts are usually taken near timberline in mountain regions. Pelt color varies in the marten, and the young from a single litter may range in color from various shades of brown to jet black, while others quite often turn out to be as red as a fox.

Like all members of the weasel family, the marten is a killer. It is also one of the few animals that can climb fast enough to catch

166

a squirrel in a tree. It feeds on mice, rabbits, birds, and will even fish for trout in some of the smaller mountain streams. It likes the taste of fish, and some martens are accidentally caught in mink sets where fish is used for bait.

Marten trapping is always a rugged occupation because of the deep snow and low temperatures where these animals are found. But after you get into the area, and get some trails laid out, the rest is rather easy. The marten is a shy animal and prefers to live away from man and all his improvements, but it has no fear of man and no suspicion at all when it comes to traps. It is one of the

Pole Set For Fisher and Marten

Bait

Traps

about 5'

few animals that will climb up on top of an uncovered trap and use it for a platform to stand on, in order to reach the bait.

Martens are travelers, and they travel in groups of about six to a dozen animals. After you get them started coming to your sets, it is no problem at all to catch every one in the group.

The marten has sharp eyes, a keen sense of smell, and is always

168

inquisitive about any unusual odor that might represent food. Since food is scarce during the winter months in areas where the marten lives, the dead of winter is the time to trap it. It will readily come to any kind of fish or flesh bait, and will follow a scent trail for several hundred yards. The odor of fresh blood seems to drive the marten almost crazy.

BAITED CUBBY   This is a favorite set for trapping marten. It can be made on the ground, out of small logs and evergreen boughs, or it can be made in the base of a hollow stump or in the end of a hollow log. Since marten live in deep snow country and new snowfalls are frequent, most trappers prefer to make their marten cubbies 4 or 5 feet off the ground and among the sheltering branches of an evergreen tree. The marten isn't particular, so make these sets wherever convenient for you. Locate two limbs on the same level, from 12 to 16 inches apart. Lay limbs and twigs across these to make a platform to hold the trap, and wire them down to keep them from falling when the animal climbs on them. Place a No. 1 or No. 1½ size trap on the platform, and hang the bait approximately 12 inches above this. Tie the trap chain to another limb, so that when the trapped animal jumps off it will hang in midair. Martens are also cannibals, and if they can reach a trapped marten the whole clan gathers and quickly devours it.

Another version of the baited cubby, one a lot of veteran trappers use, is a gallon can tacked to the side of a tree. They place the bait in the back, put the trap in the entrance, use mink or beaver scent near the set, and then they are ready for business. Canned cat food, sardines, sockeye salmon, or mackerel, mixed with glycerin, to make it sticky and keep it from freezing, all make excellent bait for the marten.

The marten is skinned cased and dried fur-side-out. Since there is very little fat on this animal, fleshing is no problem at all. The traditional way of handling marten pelts has been to skin the feet out. Use a pair of sharp wire cutters to clip the toes away from the foot, and leave the toes and claws attached to the pelt. Some buyers still want them this way while others don't, so check on this point with your buyer before skinning.

19 | The Fisher

The fisher is another tree-climbing member of the weasel family. Three times as large as the marten but not as large as the wolverine, the fisher has most of the characteristics of both. It is a wilderness animal and is found in parts of Alaska and Canada, and in some of the forests in the northeastern United States. Because few people ever see it, or even know it is around, the fisher has always been an animal of mystery.

Some early trappers thought the fisher was a member of the cat family, while others thought it was a tree-climbing fox. And many of the superstitious native trappers in northern areas thought it was a trapline thief that had been sent to punish them for breaking some taboo. Thus, the fisher grew bigger and wilder every time trappers got together and told stories about it.

Better methods of winter transportation, plus more all-weather roads leading into wilderness areas, have allowed people to get into the areas where the fisher lives and to study it in its natural habitat. This has done much to lift the veil of secrecy that formerly surrounded this seldom-seen, shy animal.

The fisher hunts in the trees for porcupines, birds, and squirrels, on the ground for rabbits and mice, and in marshy areas for muskrats, small beaver, and waterfowl. It will catch and eat fish, but it's not as fond of these as its name implies. It seems to prefer fish that comes ready cooked or out of a can, because like its smaller cousin, the marten, some of the best baits used for drawing the fisher to a set are sardines, canned cat food, sockeye salmon, and mackerel.

The female fisher is small when compared to the male. The average female weighs only 4 or 5 pounds, while some of the full-grown males tip the scales at 12 to 15 pounds. Up until the last

Ron Pittard

172

Cubby Set For Fisher

few years, the female pelt has been much more valuable and in greater demand than the larger, but coarser, pelt of the male.

Fishers breed in the early spring and a litter usually runs from three to five young. Like other members of the weasel clan, the mothers have to keep the old males away from the young ones until they are large enough to take care of themselves. Fishers, too, are cannibals and use this method of keeping their numbers under control and within the available food supply.

The fisher is not in any danger of becoming extinct—and probably never will be, because it has few natural enemies and lives so far back in the wilderness that it is not in constant contact with man—but the rugged wilderness trapper that goes after this valuable pelt is rapidly becoming a vanishing species. Even with modern methods of transportation, the weather is still cold, the snow is still deep, and trapping the fisher is a mighty hard way to earn a living.

BAITED CUBBY SET The best set for fisher is some sort of baited cubby. Since the fisher always lives in heavy snow country, the set should be placed back under the sheltering limbs of a thick evergreen tree or some other place where it will be protected from the weather. Natural crevices, back under overhanging rocks, with a steel trap or a large killer trap placed in the entrance, make an excellent location for a set for fisher.

Many trappers prefer a walk-through cubby for this animal. This is a man-made tunnel, about 6 feet long. Drive upright stakes for the sides and then roof over the entire cubby with evergreen boughs. Place a skinned beaver carcass in the middle, and place two No. 3 or No. 4 size traps in each entrance. Cover the traps with leaves or needles, and keep them inside far enough so they will be partially protected from snow. A large killer trap in each entrance, in place of the steel traps, will catch and quickly kill any fisher that tries to squeeze through it.

The fisher has a keen sense of smell, good eyesight, and, like all hungry animals, will follow a scent trail for a long distance if it thinks the trail leads to food. Use fish oil, raw beaver castor, or fox food lure to draw it into the set.

Like most long-haired furs, the fisher is skinned cased and dried fur-side-out. There are no particular problems with skinning. The pelt is easy to peel, and can be scraped right on the fur stretcher, with a dull fleshing knife. The fisher's pelt is valuable, so take extra care with the entire operation.

20 | The Nutria

The nutria (coypu) is a misplaced native of southern South America. It was brought to the United States by promoters and get-rich-quick fur farmers shortly after the time the chinchilla bubble burst. Thousands of nutria were subsequently released or escaped, and since they are very prolific, they soon became a serious nuisance.

Similar in looks and shape to an overgrown muskrat, but with coarser and longer fur, this semiaquatic rodent is as large as a medium-size beaver. When it moves into an area the area quickly becomes overcrowded, the food supply is seriously depleted, and all the other animals that depend on the same food supply either starve or have to leave. Most of the people who know the nutria, including the trapper, wish it had never moved into their part of the country.

The nutria is found in almost all of the southern states, and is now working its way up the West Coast as far as southern Washington. Shooting, trapping, and even poison haven't dented its numbers or in any way slowed its expansion. However, there may be some hope for the future. Furriers are finding more uses for the nutria's pelts, and prices are going up all the time, making it well worth trapping.

The nutria has several litters of young each year, with each

Ron Pittard

litter numbering from two to a dozen. They den in bank burrows
with underwater entrances, similar to the burrows of their larger
cousin, the beaver. Since they burrow for food, as well as a place
to live, they quickly undermine the banks and cause flooding and
erosion problems. Lowland rice farmers and cotton farmers hate
this animal because it causes them thousands of dollars of losses
each year.

176

The nutria is a nocturnal animal and does most of its feeding at night. It is a vegetarian, with most of its diet consisting of rushes, water weeds, and the bark of trees and bushes that grow along the banks. If it gets the opportunity, it will move into a stream-side garden and eat every growing plant in sight. Occasionally the nutria will also eat frogs, clams, mussels, and crawfish.

The nutria has few natural enemies. Large garfish, alligators, and turtles catch some of the young in the water, while foxes, coyotes, and bobcats grab others off the bank, but very few animals, including the otter, dare tackle a full-grown nutria. It has long, chisel-shaped teeth, like a beaver, and strong jaw muscles, which makes it well-equipped for self-defense if another animal attacks it.

A trapped nutria will also fight a trapper, so it pays to be careful. The nutria can inflict a serious wound or even take a finger completely off with one snap of its powerful jaws. The only safe time to handle the nutria is after it is dead.

The nutria is trapped similar to the muskrat but larger size traps are used since it's a larger and much stronger animal. The nutria is easy to trap, and even an inexperienced youngster has no trouble at all in trapping all the nutria that he can take care of. The Bank Pocket Set, exactly like that for the muskrat, but with No. 2 or No. 3 size traps, is one of the best sets for these animals. Use muskrat food lure for scent and an apple or carrot for bait. If at all possible, use a drowning rig—with the one-way slide on the wire—similar to sets made for beaver. But if the water is too shallow for drowning, use a stake to hold the trapped animal in the water.

Large killer traps, set in den entrances, are also very good sets for nutria. When using these traps, you have no problems with drowning.

The pelt of the nutria, which is skinned cased and dried fur-side-in, resembles that of the opossum. Pelt quality is judged by the under fur. This is the only fur-bearing animal skin that is cut along the back during the processing, because the fur on the sides and the belly of a nutria is thicker and of a much higher quality.

21 | The Opossum

The opossum may be considered one of North America's most remarkable animals, simply from the fact that this slow-moving, rather dull-witted animal has been able to survive at all. This cat-size tree-climber is a living example of ancient history. The opossum seems to live by the theory that if "You can't lick them, join them." Instead of having to move out when people move in, the opossum has moved right in with them.

Many opossums are found even in our largest cities. They prowl by night and eat out of garbage cans and snatch leftover food in dog and cat pans. They will live under your house or in your garage, and you may never know they are around unless you happen to see one accidentally.

The opossum was built for survival—but not much of anything else. Nature seems to have shortchanged them when it comes to such things as speed, thinking ability, and a glamorous pelt. On the other hand, the opossum is endowed with some traits that no other animal on the North American continent is equipped with. And each of these additions has helped this mild-mannered, awkward animal survive, and increase both its range and numbers, while other, much more "sophisticated" animals have had to give up the struggle and have fallen by the wayside.

The opossum is very adaptable and can live almost anywhere.

It prefers to live in wooded areas in more temperate climates, but its range has expanded to include Oregon and Washington and the southern part of British Columbia.

Because of a body odor that is offensive to both man and animal, the opossum has few natural enemies, and very few animals and predatory birds ever get hungry enough to eat it. Although "baked possum and sweet potatoes" was a popular dish during the

Ron Pittard

Depression, I sincerely doubt if anyone would have preferred this rather gamy dish, if adequate amounts of beef or pork had been available.

The opossum's diet is varied and it will eat almost anything: fruit, vegetables, nesting birds, mice, rabbits, fish, and frogs. It will even make a raid on a hen roost when it gets the opportunity. If fresh meat is not available, the opossum will eat carrion.

The principal reason the opossum has been able to do so well under adverse conditions is because it is a prolific marsupial. Marsupials bear premature young that live and are nourished in a pouch in the abdomen of the female. Wherever the mother goes, the young go along, and she is always right there to protect them.

The opossum has a usable thumb and fingers on each of its four feet, plus a long ratlike prehensile tail that can be used for grasping and wrapping around limbs when climbing. And while it isn't as fast in a tree as a cat, it can climb fast enough to escape from most of its enemies.

Most opossums live and hunt in wooded areas, where in case of danger they can quickly climb a tree. If they get caught on the ground, their main defense is to put up no resistance at all. The opossum gets a silly grin on its face, drools a little, rolls its eyes back in its head, tucks its feet and tail under to protect its belly, and rolls over and plays dead. After its enemy gets tired of mauling it and leaves, the opossum will slowly open its eyes, look around, and if the coast is clear make a quick dash for the nearest tree. This animal is tenacious and tough, and even a dog can chew on it and do very little damage. The opossum can shrug off brutal treatment that would kill a more sensitive animal in a few minutes.

Under ordinary circumstances, opossums aren't much for fighting, but they do have a big mouth, strong jaw muscles, and sharp teeth. Occasionally, when a female has young in her pouch she

Sets For Opossum

Stump Set

Bait

Den Set

Cubby Set

forgets all about being docile, and if some larger animal happens to attack her, she will put up quite a battle. When she does bite, she bites deep and then hangs on and keeps right on chewing.

The opossum dens in hollow trees, logs, stumps, animal burrows, and under barns and other farm buildings. In more moderate climates, they may have two litters of from four to twelve young. When born, the young aren't even as large as a honeybee. They climb into the pouch and attach themselves to a nipple and usually stay there for four to six weeks. By this time, things in the pouch are getting a little crowded, and the larger and stronger babies push the weak ones out. Usually only four to six survive. These stay with their mother for another two or three months, and then break away from the family group to start families of their own.

182

The Opossum

The opossum fears neither man nor traps, and even an inexperienced youngster can easily catch this animal. Use box traps when trapping near inhabited areas, and either steel traps or small killer traps when trapping in places where dogs or cats will not be caught.

Traps set in den entrances are good, but probably the best set for this unwary animal is one that involves some kind of bait. Since the opossum always seems to be hungry and is never too particular about what it feeds on, almost any kind of meat, either fresh or rotten, will draw it to a set. Place the meat in a cubby or a crevice in the rocks, in an old stump, or even hang it at the base of a tree. Use No. 1 or No. 1½ size steel traps, or one of the small-size killer traps. Wire it securely and cover it lightly. If there is an opossum in the area, chances are good that it will be in it the next time you check your traps.

The opossum is skinned cased and dried fur-side-in. When skinning, take special care with the female because her pouch is tender and will tear easily. This is one animal that has a lot of fat, so you will have to pull its pelt on the fleshing beam or pole and work down with the fleshing knife. Scrape off all excess flesh and fat, but not so close that the hair roots are exposed. Wipe off all grease and then tack the pelt on the stretcher to dry.

No one ever got rich from trapping opossums but many youngsters from rural areas make a lot of their winter spending money from the sale of "possum" pelts. The opossum may be stupid and awkward but in spite of that, nature made this animal to last. It will probably still be here—grinning, and doing whatever it is that opossums do—long after the last man has gone from the earth.

22 | The Skunk

The skunk, a medium-size member of the weasel family, is an animal with a bad reputation—and most of it undeserved. Contrary to popular opinion, skunks are not mean, they are not dirty, and above all, they don't go around spraying their nose-searing odor at everything in sight. These gentle and nonaggressive animals are neat and clean in their personal habits, and neither their bodies nor their dens ever have more than a slight odor about them, unless some man or animal threatens their lives. And even then, they use their powerful spray sparingly because they know that their ammunition supply is limited to three or four magnum-size blasts. Since they are usually too fat for running, and not much for fighting, they have to hoard this spray until the enemy gets in close; otherwise they are completely helpless.

Although the skunk has one of the most durable and beautiful pelts of all the North American fur-bearers, most North American women wouldn't wear a garment made from these glossy, black and white pelts if someone were to pay them to do so. European women, on the other hand, know a good thing when they see it. And it's a darn good thing that they do, because U.S. trappers have to depend on them for most of the market.

The skunk prefers to live closer to civilization than to the wilderness. Just about every farm and even the suburbs of our

Ron Pittard

largest cities seem to be overrun with a thriving population of these unpopular animals. Since no one seems to want the skunk around, almost every landowner will be eager to grant permission for someone to trap it.

For obvious reasons, the skunk has few natural enemies and little fear of man or traps. It always seems to be hungry and will go out of its way to investigate any odor that represents food. Trapping this animal is easy; the main problem in skunk trapping is to get the animal out of the trap without getting its powerful odor all over you. The best way that I have found to hold this awesome smell to a minimum is to shoot the skunk through the ear, leave it in the trap overnight, and then take it out the next day. Use gloves when handling the trap and the animal. Field skin it, and then drop the pelt in a plastic bag for transportation back to your home base.

Skunks are nocturnal animals and do most of their hunting at night. They feed on mice, rabbits, birds, insects, fruit, and berries. They will go out of their way for a chance to clean out a hen coop of both eggs and chickens. And when they start these nighttime forays, they will return to the scene of the crime at least once a week, until the farmer runs out of chickens or finds some way to stop them.

The skunk semihibernates during the coldest months of winter, usually in a burrow or rocky ledge that faces south. Whenever there happens to be a bright, sunshiny day, anywhere from two to a dozen of these animals will come out and lie in the sun. These winter dens can be located and identified by tracks, droppings, and grass pulled into the entrance.

Skunks are found in almost every section of the United States and in the southern part of Canada. They come in various shapes and sizes, from the small spotted skunk that is about the size of a mink, to the large broad-stripe that may weigh as much as 10 or 12 pounds. All have the scent glands under their tail, and can throw a jet of this powerful deterrent for a distance of 10 to 12 feet. If an unlucky trapper happens to get hit by it, it can temporarily blind him, make him extremely sick, and assure him of being shunned by society for at least several days.

The skunk is one of the easiest of the fur-bearers to trap. Sets made in the entrance to the winter dens are very effective. When you locate one of these dens, make one or two cubby-type bait sets in the vicinity. Birds, rabbits, or fish make excellent bait for

Den OR Baited Cubby

the skunk. A bait, tied to a stump, tree, or fence post, with a No. 1 or No. 1½ size trap set directly under it, also makes a good set for these unwary animals.

STONE CIRCLE SET   This is one of the most effective sets for skunks. Make a rough circle with bucket-size stones. Place a large bait in the center—a skinned skunk carcass seems to be best—and cover the bait with grass to keep it out of sight of predatory birds. Set small steel traps in the 4- to 6-inch space between the stones. Tie the traps to a short fence post, or something similar, for a drag. This will let the trapped skunk leave the immediate area, but still hang up in the nearest patch of brush. When made near a den, this set will take as many as six skunks in a single night.

The skunk is skinned cased and dried fur-side-in. It peels easy, but be extremely cautious when skinning around the scent glands near the vent. Strip the tail from the bone, and then use the small blade of a sharp knife and split the tail to the tip.

The skunk is a fat animal and all the excess flesh and fat must be removed. Pull the pelt on a beam or pole and scrape with the fleshing knife. Wipe off all excess grease (be sure that you get it

187

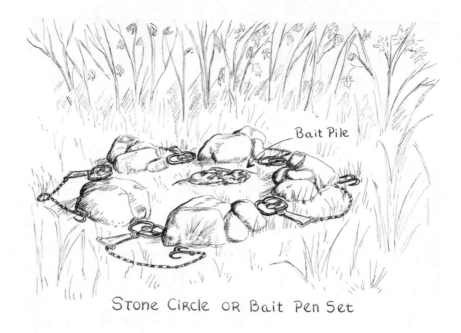

Bait Pile

Stone Circle or Bait Pen Set

off the fur), and then wipe every two or three days while the pelt is drying. If you happen to get any odor on your hands or clothing, first wash them in tomato juice, then follow with strong soap and hot water. Even this won't get all the odor, but it will get most of it; a lot of elapsed time and fresh air will get the rest.

23 | The Weasel

Of the thirty-six species and subspecies of the weasel family scattered all over North America, the smallest member of this large clan of killers seems to be the most bloodthirsty of the entire lot. With a body length of 6 to 10 inches, and never more than a few ounces in weight, this pint-size bundle of fury has been known to attack animals as large as a horse. Surprisingly, when it does launch an attack on a much larger animal, the little brown weasel usually comes out the winner.

With a shrill scream of rage that throws its opponent off guard, this tiny killer strikes like a snake—and every time it hits, the fur or feathers fly. Surprised, confused, and often scared half out of its wits by these buzz-saw tactics, the larger animal usually forgets all about being brave and leaves in a hurry. It is a good thing that the weasel is small. If it were as large as a raccoon or otter, no man or animal would be safe in the woods.

The weasel likes the taste of fresh blood and prefers to kill its own food. Most of its fare is made up of mice, birds, rats, and rabbits. It likes to kill—just for the thrill of killing—and if it gets the chance to slip into a hen coop, it will really go on a blood-letting spree.

The largest member of the family is the long-tailed weasel, with a full-grown male—tail and all—reaching a length of about

Weasel.

16 inches. The short-tailed weasel reaches a total length of about
12 inches, and the smallest member, the least weasel, never gets
much larger than a mouse. In northern areas, all weasels are
brown during the summer but they turn white in winter, with a
tiny black tip on their tail. Known to the fur trade as ermine, the
prime winter pelts are the only ones that have any value.

190

The Weasel

The weasel is a traveler. It has good eyesight, a keen sense of smell, and a built-in curiosity that causes it to investigate any scent trail that its tiny nose happens to encounter. And since it has no fear of man or traps, and it refuses to admit that anything could possibly harm it, all in all I'd say the weasel is a rather easy animal to trap.

In warmer areas, the weasel has two or three litters of from four to eight young each year. Since they are such vicious animals, they have few natural enemies. Horned owls do take a few, but most of the larger predators have found that they stand to lose more than they can possibly gain. The weasel also has scent glands, similar to those of the skunk. Therefore, even if they did kill it, very few animals would ever eat the weasel.

The weasel lives in the wilderness, the deserts, the mountains, and along the fringes of the southern swamps, in rocky ledges, hollow logs, post piles, and under farm buildings. Since it does most of its hunting at night, very few people ever see it. Most of its hunting is done on the ground, but it is also an excellent climber and preys on young squirrels and birds in their nests.

Almost any fresh meat makes a good bait for weasel. My own preference is either fresh fish or liver. Place the bait in a hollow log or cubby and put a small trap in the entrance. Use the No. 0 or No. 1 size steel traps, or one of the smaller killer traps. Mink scent, raw weasel musk, or even cheap perfume will draw weasels to the set.

A favorite set with many trappers is to wire an old-fashioned wooden-base rat trap to the bottom of a fence post or tree. Tie a thumb-size chunk of fresh liver to the trigger. When the weasel tries to take the bait, the trap snaps shut and kills it instantly.

Weasels are skinned cased and stretched fur-side-in, and since there is no fat on this tiny pelt, fleshing is never a problem. Blood stains white pelts, so be sure and wash it off before skinning.

191

Ron Pittard

Ermine.

Weasels are plentiful in most areas and are easy to trap. Although no one I know has ever made a fortune trapping weasels, setting a few weasel traps, along with the rest of my trapline, always seemed an easy way of making a few extra dollars. And while a single pelt never brings much, it can add up if you multiply it by fifty or sixty.

Trapping Ethics

Fur trapping is one of our oldest occupations. And the trapper must have been doing at least a few things right for the last million years or so, because according to statistics, there are more trappers now—and also more animals to trap—than ever before in history. This should be living proof that the trapper has always been a good conservationist. Traditionally he has not only taken pretty good care of himself and his family, but also of the fur-bearing animals that he had to depend on to furnish his winter's income. But past history is soon forgotten. Times change, and the one-time independent fur trapper has had to change with them. And unless he is willing to change even more in the near future, the fur trapper himself is in danger of becoming a vanishing species.

The old days are gone. And unless we admit it to ourselves and accept the added responsibilities placed on us by modern times and expanding civilization, the current crop of fur trappers will soon go the way of the Mountain Men. This can happen unless we come out of the bushes and stand up and be counted. How can this be done? Here are a few suggestions.

Join your local trapper's association. Not only pay your dues, but make it a special point to attend all the meetings.

Get to know your local game warden and also other game management people in your area.

Obey all trapping rules and regulations. And if you think changes are needed, make suggestions.

Get to know the landowners in your area and obtain permission before setting any traps.

Avoid setting traps in any area where domestic animals might be caught. If you do have to trap these areas in order to remove nuisance animals, use box-traps, so that all other animals can be released unharmed.

Always check your traps on a regular basis. Each day, and early in the morning, if possible. And never trap any kind of animal where the public can see it.

Go out of your way to help landowners with predator problems. But when you do it, be sure you do it in compliance with all local rules and regulations.

Consider fur as a crop that also belongs to future generations. Trap only the surplus animals. Trap these when their pelts are prime, and always take good care of the furs that you catch.

Use drowning methods whenever you can. Use killer traps whenever possible. Never use large steel traps for small or medium-sized animals. And use traps with off-set jaws for the larger predators.

Write letters to the people that represent you on both state and federal levels. Make suggestions; quite often, they can be of great help.

Teach youngsters how to trap. Show them how to be good trappers. Stress sportsmanship and responsibilities and be sure that they understand it. These youngsters are the trappers of tomorrow. Any time we spend with them is our investment in the future.

Conclusion

Ever since movies, TV, and children's books started the un-realistic humanization of animals, the fur trapper has been under increasing criticism from many so-called animal protectionist groups that have little knowledge of the complex world of nature. Many people in these groups are sincere in their belief that the world would be a much nicer place to live in if no bird or animal was ever hurt or killed. But these people are simply not realistic, and are being swayed by their emotions. Since they have little, if any, contact with the outdoor world, they are being brainwashed by promoters and fast-buck artists who are getting rich off the money these compassionate people are contributing for the wel-fare of wildlife. Instead of helping, they are actually hurting the animals they would like to protect.

As an outdoorsman, a long-time student of nature, and a fur trapper, I know that the population numbers of animals must be managed and controlled—for the good of both man and animal. And while my views on the subject might not always be exactly the same as that of a trained naturalist, a wildlife biologist, or the professionals in charge of state and federal game and wildlife management programs, we agree wholeheartedly that the only possible way to protect all forms of wildlife and preserve it for the future is to manage its population numbers through con-trolled hunting and trapping.

We can pass and enforce laws against trespassing by people, and if I kill a farmer's sheep or cattle, I face a stiff fine and will probably land in jail. Or if I cut his trees, drain his ponds, or destroy his crops, the penalty would be severe. But an animal has no concern for property lines or the lives of others in the world of nature. All birds and animals take what they can get, and they get it any way they possibly can. If a man or animal stands in the way, they have to step aside or suffer the consequences.

Survival of the fittest is the supreme law in the world of nature, and no set of laws passed by man will ever change or repeal it. This is the way it has always been, and we would be foolish to expect it to change in the future. So instead of trying to change the habits of nature, let's try to change the habits of people instead.

At the present time, millions of hard-earned dollars and count-less valuable man-hours are being wasted by the protectionist groups on one side and the outdoor groups on the other. As a whole, wildlife is the loser. We must quit wasting this valuable time and money. First, we have to get rid of the promoters and fast-buck artists on both sides and then we must develop new and better methods of game management, devise new and more hu-mane traps and control methods, and purchase more land for game preserves and sanctuaries, where animals can live out their lives without being bothered. Landowners should be compen-sated for wildlife damage, but in return for this protection, we must insist that they allow competent people to control wildlife numbers before damage occurs.

Humans have to come first, but it would be a sorry world in-deed if there was no room left for wildlife. Let's approach these problems in a sensible manner, work out some realistic answers, and strive to make it a better world, where both man and animal can live in harmony.

INDEX

INDEX

199